FORBIDDEN

BRITAIN

FORBIDDEN BRITAIN

STEVE HUMPHRIES
AND PAMELA GORDON

BBC Books

With love to Sophie, Anna and Sally
STEVE HUMPHRIES

For Ashley
PAMELA GORDON

This book is published to accompany the
television series entitled *Forbidden Britain*

Published by BBC Books,
a division of BBC Enterprises Limited,
Woodlands, 80 Wood Lane,
London W12 0TT

First published 1994
© Stephen Humphries and Pamela Gordon

ISBN 0 563 36974 4

Designed by Judith Robertson
Set in Goudy by Goodfellow & Egan Ltd, Cambridge
Printed and Bound in Great Britain by Clays Ltd, St Ives PLC,
Colour separation by Technik Ltd, Berkhamsted,
Jacket printed by Belmont Press Ltd, Northampton

Right: Policemen dismantling a barricade after the Battle of Cable Street in London's East End in 1936.

CONTENTS

INTRODUCTION

On Thursday 12 June 1919, the main story in the *South Wales News* was of race riots that had occurred the night before.

"The white versus black feud has extended to Cardiff and Barry. In a series of riots last night two men were killed and sixteen injured. One of these, a discharged soldier with a record of four years war service, was fatally stabbed in Beverley Street, Cadoxton, Barry. The alleged assailant, a coloured man, is now under arrest. The affair aroused the anger of the white people, notably ex-soldiers and sailors, who paraded the streets in an ugly temper, seeking 'blacks' and window smashing where the latter were suspected to lurk. The police in large force kept the crowd moving. Order was not restored until the early hours of this morning. An extraordinary colour riot also broke out at Cardiff late last night. The negroes used revolvers and razors freely. The police leading, the mob made after the blacks who vanished into a house. Forcing an entry, the officers, after a violent struggle, made several arrests. The house was subsequently set on fire and burnt out. Three shots were fired at the South Wales News *representative."*

Riots in the city streets are often thought of as something new. Surely they could never have happened in Britain – supposedly one of the most law-abiding countries in the world – during the first half of this century? Major civil disturbances and violent clashes were in fact much more common than has previously been thought. Riots are just one of many of today's major social problems which have a secret past. Juvenile crime, extra-marital affairs, government work schemes for the unemployed, child sexual abuse and homelessness were also part of the British way of life long before the last war.

Much has remained hidden because of Government censorship of information and ideas considered to be damaging or dangerous. Feature film or newsreel coverage of all the issues we explore was either banned or closely controlled. The press did cover subjects like riots, juvenile crime and affairs in

A publicity shot from the 1923 film *Human Wreckage,* which examined the problem of drug abuse.

some detail, but the reporting was often extremely biased and distorted. In the race riots of May and June 1919, for example, the overwhelming reaction of the press was to blame Britain's black community for the violence directed at them. The most taboo subjects like incest and child sexual abuse were considered so shocking they were rarely reported on or even spoken about.

The aim of this book – and the television series it accompanies – is to chronicle the secret history of what was 'forbidden Britain'. The most vivid and effective way to document our secret past is through personal testimony. In writing this book we corresponded with or spoke to around 2500 people born between the 1890s and the 1940s. Most wrote to us in answer to our call for memories, published in local newspapers all over Britain. By drawing on this material we have tried to provide new information and insights into the darker side of life in Britain during the first half of the twentieth century. The book portrays the lives of those stigmatized as delinquents, rioters, mistresses, tramps and the long-term unemployed. Their experiences vividly illuminate how behaviour condemned at the time as ignorant and immoral was often a discriminating response to inequality, injustice and discrimination. We also tell the harrowing and deeply moving story of girls and boys who were sexually abused in the past. Their memories paint a graphic picture of the fear and violence in which most child sexual abuse was rooted.

Each chapter explores a particular theme previously hidden from history. We have tried to capture the uniqueness and individuality of each person's story by quoting them at some length. The context for their personal testimonies is provided by an introductory overview to each chapter. The voices heard in the book are those of around thirty people who contacted us and whom we interviewed in depth. Most of the interviews were filmed for the television series. Through them we hear, for the first time, the authentic voice of 'forbidden Britain'.

1

RUNNING WILD
DELINQUENCY

Glasgow in the 1920s and 1930s had the disturbing reputation of a city swarming with razor-wielding gangs of youths. Gangs like the Billy Boys, the Carlton Entry, the South Side Stickers and the Beehive seemed to be openly flouting the law with their street fighting, vandalism and crime. There had been similar fears in other cities down the century. In the early 1900s there was deep concern about a South London gang, the Hooligans. 'Hooligan' quickly became a generic term of abuse for any rebellious activity in which young people were involved. In Manchester there was a series of panics between the 1880s and the 1920s about a succession of violent street gangs – the Scuttlers, the Ikey Boys and the Napoo. Public fears were stirred up by lurid and sensational press reports. But the existence of these rebellious and semi-criminal gangs was real enough, even though their violence might be exaggerated. They were endemic in poor working-class communities all over Britain, in which it was a fact of life that many children and young people would drift in and out of 'delinquent' or 'semi-delinquent' gangs, especially during their teenage years.

Children became involved with street gangs from a very young age. Working-class children spent much of their free time on the streets – their homes were so small and overcrowded that they had little or no space to play indoors. On the streets they enjoyed a culture quite independent from the adult world. The street became a stage for a welter of running, chasing, ball-bouncing and skipping games. Adults found many of the games annoying, anti-social or dangerous. Windows were occasionally smashed in street games and pranks like 'Knock Out Ginger' – knocking on doors and running away – were designed to irritate grown-ups. The children and young people often formed themselves into gangs which were highly territorial, frequently taking the name of their own street or neighbourhood. There would be sporadic fights

A gang of street urchins in the
East End of London around the
turn of the century. Children
like these often became involved
in crime at an early age.

between rival gangs in which every self-respecting boy would be expected to take part. Fists, boots, sticks, stones and bricks were the weapons. But the conflicts were highly ritualized and most combatants escaped with just a few cuts and bruises.

Pilfering and petty theft were extremely common amongst poor children on the streets. Driven by hunger and with no money in their pockets, their main targets were the sweet shop, the greengrocer or the market stall. Very often these minor crimes would be elaborately executed by a small gang – each with a part to play as look-outs or decoys – with the spoils shared later on in a safe place. Sometimes the children stole food and fuel for the family. They would take coal from pitheads, wood from timber yards and vegetables from farmers' fields. Most of the poorest parents turned a blind eye to this kind of property theft or even openly welcomed the bounty when their children brought it home. Much of this crime was directed towards small traders and the property-owning classes. There was certainly little to steal from ordinary families in a poor working-class area before the last war – many happily left their doors unlocked all day and night.

Most of this crime committed by children and younger teenagers was hidden from police records or criminal statistics. Most offences were dealt with on the spot by the policeman on his beat and were not followed by any prosecution – there would be immediate retribution in the form of a 'backhander' and the offender would then be frog-marched back to return the stolen goods and the aggrieved party would have their chance to punish the child. The parents would also be warned, which might lead to another beating – if only for getting caught. Consequently even in the poorest areas during the inter-war years it was rare for more than one in every hundred children to be prosecuted each year by the police. But if the multitude of hidden and undetected crimes was to be taken into account then, as criminologist Cyril Burt put it in his book *The Young Delinquent* written in 1925, 'one could expand the percentage to almost any degree. Delinquency shadows the life of the city child.'

The crimes of older gangs of youths were taken more seriously by the police and if caught they would invariably be punished. Some of these gangs like the Glasgow Billy Boys or the Birmingham Peaky Blinders possessed

A Scottish policeman reprimanding two children for stealing turnips. Many poor children were driven by hunger to eat raw vegetables taken from farmers' fields.

armouries of dangerous weapons such as spiked knuckledusters, sharpened bicycle chains, knives, razors, coshes and, in a few cases, pistols. Conflicts between gangs renowned for their 'tough' reputations could be very bloody, occasionally resulting in serious injury or death. For example, in the Albert Street brawl of 1928 between the Glasgow gangs the South Side Stickers and the Carlton Entry, Tate of the Carlton Gang was killed. Territorial and gang rivalries could be further inflamed by differences of nationality and religion. Every year in Belfast, Glasgow and Liverpool the mass parades on Orange Day and St Patrick's Day would be followed by violent fights between Protestant and Catholic gangs.

Property crime committed by gangs of older teenagers was most common in areas of high unemployment and peaked at moments when there were large numbers on the dole. Favourite targets were shops and warehouses: booze, cigarettes, food and clothing would be sold secretly or kept for the gang. The Beehive Gang in the Glasgow Gorbals – many of whose members were unemployed – was well known for its criminal activities in the twenties. It was also one of the first gangs involved in joy-riding on motor bikes and in motor cars.

Girls and young women played only a minor role in street gangs. There were a few all-female gangs like the Check Skirt Gang – a semi-criminal gang of teenage girls operating in Paddington during the First World War. But generally families exercised much stricter control over the movements of daughters ensuring they were more home-based and less likely to get into trouble with the law. Criminal prosecutions against young women for theft were a fraction of the rate amongst young men. The annual Criminal Statistics for the 1930s reveal that only one girl for every thirteen boys was prosecuted.

The main anxiety about delinquency amongst girls and young women focused around sex outside marriage. During the first decades of the century there was a cluster of concerns which revolved around the new, liberated woman, the massive increase in venereal disease and the rise of under-age sex, all of which seemed to threaten the stability of family life. Sex before marriage was still widely seen as immoral and single girls who indulged were branded 'amateur prostitutes'. But official attempts to protect young women from the dangers of sex actually had the effect of criminalizing them. Some young women whose only 'crime' was to have sex were sent to approved schools or

A publicity photograph from *Children on Trial*, a film made in 1946 about juvenile delinquency.

other institutions for young offenders – some were even put away in mental handicap hospitals under the wide-ranging Mental Deficiency Act of 1913.

The biggest panic about sexual behaviour was triggered by the 'dope girls' in the early 1920s. There was a fashion for the use of opium and cocaine, both of which had recently been made illegal, especially amongst young people in London's West End night clubs. The opium dens of Chinatown in London and Liverpool – where Chinese seamen and dockers had for many years smoked opium – also became a focus for official concern, particularly as there were fears that droves of white girls were being lured into these exotic places to be seduced by men from other races. Drug use came to be seen as part of a crisis of young womanhood. Fischer and Dubois wrote in their book *Sexual History of the World War* (1937):

> "The numerical discrepancy between the two sexes on the home front (during the Great War) produced the logical consequence that, in a great many cases, a number of women would expect sexual satisfaction from one man. Frequently parties were organised, consisting of a number of women and only one or two men, and, generally after prolonged bouts of drinking combined with drug taking the worst sexual orgies took place. Cocaine addicts, losing all self control and all moral sense, would practise every variant of 'group love' which sometimes took such disgusting forms that it would be impossible to describe them in a scientific work."

But the drug habit was never anywhere near as widespread or as far reaching in its effects on sexual behaviour as was imagined in sensational press reports and in popular histories of the time. In fact it was largely restricted – at least amongst women – to a small group of actresses, dancers and prostitutes in the capital, and the girlfriends of early drug barons like 'Brilliant' Chang.

There was little recorded 'delinquency' amongst middle- and upper-class young people during the first half of this century. This reflects a real difference in law-breaking between the classes. Well-to-do children were usually controlled to a far greater extent by adults, they spent much more time at home or at school, and they had less need to steal. Nevertheless there was also much middle-class 'delinquency' hidden from the official records. The authorities turned a blind eye to violence at rags, rugger matches and in town-and-gown fights which sometimes erupted into pitched battles in university towns like Oxford and Cambridge. These were usually just dismissed as 'high spirits' and a healthy expression of manliness. Even the train-spotting craze –

especially popular amongst middle-class boys between the 1930s and the 1950s – produced much semi-criminal activity. Boys would throw stones at engines, trespass on the tracks playing dangerous games, ride on trains without tickets, vandalize coaches and generally cause a nuisance at stations. Train-spotters were banned from the platforms of a number of main-line stations. If caught, however, they usually escaped with a telling off or a clout from railway staff.

The traditional method for dealing with children and young people who were arrested and actually prosecuted was extremely punitive. There was the short, sharp shock of a whipping. In 1917 almost 5000 of those found guilty by the juvenile courts were birched. Then there was imprisonment, sometimes with hard labour – still used as a deterrent for a small minority of teenage offenders during the inter-war years. From Victorian times onwards a range of institutions was specially developed to deal with young offenders. They were sent to reformatories, industrial schools and training-ships, which by the 1900s housed around 25 000 delinquent boys and girls. However, attempts at reform in these places were extremely harsh. The staff wielded absolute power over the inmates and set about the task of character reformation with enthusiasm. Strict regimes were established, revolving around early rising, cold baths, drill, long hours of tedious manual labour, enforced silence, military discipline and, above all, severe punishments.

In the early years of the century there were new initiatives to create more effective reformatory institutions for young offenders. Hardened offenders aged between sixteen and twenty-one were sent to borstal for periods of two or three years. Here there was a new emphasis on the house system and team games – borrowed from the public schools – to try to encourage discipline and *esprit de corps*. By the late 1930s there were around 2000 inmates of borstals. These institutions boasted that half of all the boys and girls who passed through were not re-convicted within five years. Younger offenders were sent to approved schools – an amalgamation of the old reformatories and industrial schools. Here greater efforts were made to provide moral training and useful work skills for the inmates and to use less corporal punishment.

Despite these changes the young working-class rebels put away in these institutions, whether it was a training-ship or borstal, generally found them very oppressive. Many tried to escape. 'Scarpering' was a recurrent feature of institutional life. But few attempts at escape were successful. The boys and girls were hindered by their uniform, which was conspicuous and easily identified, by their lack of money, and by their ignorance of local geography. (They were

A scene set in an opium den
from the film *The Dividend*
made in 1920.

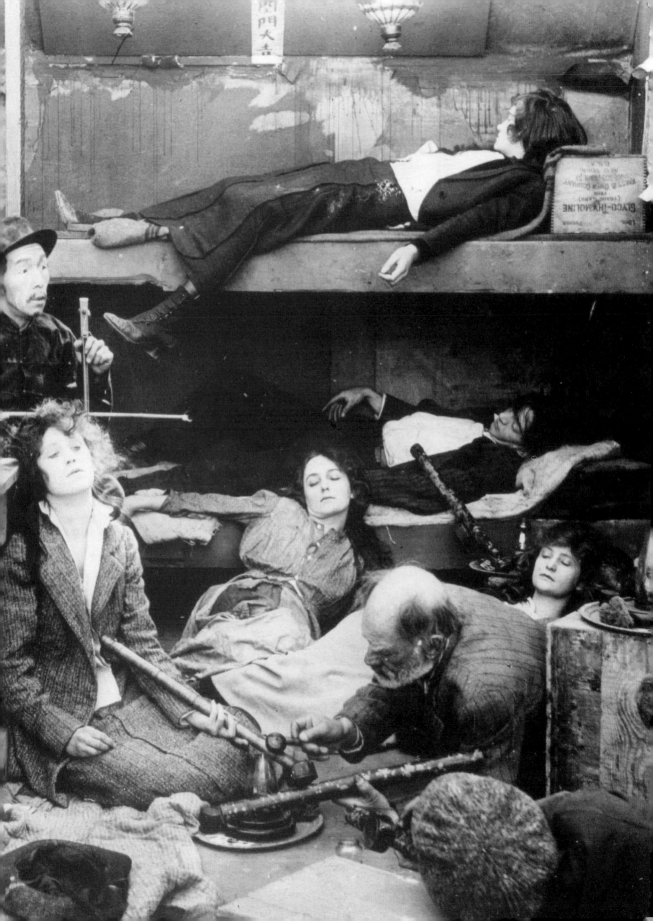

rarely allowed outside the reformatory grounds and were normally sent long distances away from their homes.) Those who escaped for long periods had to steal to survive and often committed more serious crimes than they had been put away for in the first place. However, most were quickly arrested and returned to face what was intended as a deterrent against future escape attempts – a public flogging before the assembled inmates.

One of the biggest changes in the treatment of young offenders was probation, first introduced in 1907. By the 1930s around half of all young people under seventeen found guilty by the juvenile courts were put on probation. The use of probation officers to supervise and control young offenders in the community meant that the overall numbers sent to reformatory institutions gradually decreased. Probation was also often preferred to birching and by the mid-1930s birching had reduced to around 200 cases a year. Another effect of probation was to increase the overall numbers of children and young people prosecuted. Whereas in the past there had been immediate retribution on the street for children involved in petty crimes, now there was a new trend. Police and social workers were more likely to press charges against children who had broken the law in the knowledge that the likely outcome would be a probation order – far less drastic than a birching or sending a child to an institution. The numbers of young people dealt with by the juvenile courts increased year after year from around 11 000 in 1929 to 30 000 by 1939. However, some saw the increase as a major cause for concern and evidence that young people were treated too softly. There were calls for a return to the birch even in the 1930s.

The Second World War brought with it a substantial increase in juvenile crime. Censorship of information about looting, pilfering and property crime on the home front – which was strictly enforced during the early years of the war – meant that this explosion of delinquency remained largely hidden. The number of young people found guilty by the juvenile courts rose to a peak of more than 43 000 in 1941. The increase was greatest for under fourteen-year-olds, amongst whom crime rates soared by almost 50 per cent compared to just before the war. This dramatic rise in delinquency came as no surprise to the courts. It mirrored the big increase in juvenile crime that had occurred during the First World War. The key factors were thought to be the absence of so many fathers called up to the front and a depleted police force. Although there were reserve policemen they were for the most part old, untrained and largely ineffective. The opportunities for crime in the Second World War were further

A gang of unemployed youths loitering on a street corner in the 1930s.
Lack of money, boredom and frustration sometimes led young men like these
to turn to crime.

increased by the black-out and the Blitz: many left their homes and shops every night to sleep in the shelters, an open invitation to the young criminal. In the aftermath of the bombings, possessions – including valuable ration books – were strewn everywhere, offering rich pickings for looters. Blitzed homes and streets also encouraged vandalism with children smashing windows, throwing bricks and setting fire to derelict buildings.

Evacuation, the closing of many schools and youth clubs during the Blitz and the increased employment of married women in war work all added to the disruption of the normal routine, reducing adult control over children and young people. The courts responded by bringing back the birch. The number of birchings inflicted on boys under fourteen increased from 58 in 1939 to 531 in 1941.

The government aggravated the problem of delinquency at the outset of war by releasing all the inmates of borstal who had served more than six months of their sentence. Two-thirds of the borstal population – 1677 boys and 118 girls – were discharged. It was assumed that they would want to do their bit for king and country. In fact many returned to a life of crime, in which there was more chance of success than before the war. Those who were conscripted deserted in large numbers. They formed the rump of the 'deserter' problem, a major headache for the armed forces hushed up at the time. There were more than 75 000 army court martial convictions for 'absence' or 'desertion' between 1939 and 1944. Army surveys showed that those most likely to desert were those aged twenty or below – especially those with a criminal record. More than anyone else they felt they had nothing to fight for.

In the 1950s came a new youth rebellion in the form of Teddy boys and Teddy girls. They quickly gained a frightening reputation for gang fights, rock-and-roll cinema riots, vandalism and street robberies. The Teds, with their long drape jackets, duck-tail haircuts and 'brothel creeper' shoes became folk devils, targets for hysterical attacks by politicians, the press and the police. The new generation of 'teenagers', as they came to be called, seemed to pose a threat to the British way of life itself. It was as if there had never before been a problem of juvenile delinquency.

Commentators missed the continuity between the Teds and previous 'delinquent' gangs. What was different though was that this was the first national cult which emerged from working-class youth, made possible by commercial television and the new music and fashion industries aimed at them. In the past, young people's rebellion had been rooted in local street gangs. Now with money to spend – in an era of full employment and greater affluence – the rebellion against adult authority took a more stylized form. Rebellious youth had a uniform that could be recognized in every town and city. But at root the rebellion was still all about anger, boredom, frustration and kicking against oppressive adults. These feelings were experienced by working-class young people in the 1950s just as they had been by their parents and grandparents before them.

LARRY RANKIN

Larry was born in 1912 in the Glasgow Gorbals. His father was a warehouseman and conscientious objector. Larry had two brothers and two sisters. He left school when he was fourteen and worked as an apprentice boilermaker. When he had completed his apprenticeship he was dismissed. He was one of the leading members of the Beehive Gang and turned to crime whilst unemployed. He served several prison sentences for minor property crimes. He later became a long-distance lorry driver. He had two daughters and now lives on the west coast of Scotland with his wife.

"Thistle Street was the heart of the Gorbals. It was a very depressed area at the time, it was rat-infested, bug-infested. You were unemployed. You were wearing old worn-out clothes. That was just life. We were all young fellows, we had nothing to do except stand at the corner stamping our feet. It was lack of money that was the trouble unless you wanted to live and crawl on your hands and knees and go about begging. And as you grew older you looked around and wanted to get something for yoursel', wanted to go further.

The Beehive Boys was a gang, the sons of working-class men that had been persecuted for years, perhaps been in the army, soldiers that had been told that they were returning to a land fit for heroes to live in, and then they found out that that was a lie. They were devastated because they got nothing, so the Beehive Boys they looked around them and they decided that they'd have to do something for the poor themselves.

We used to choose say a warehouse where we knew we could get something or maybe a shop which was a bit out of the way like, just smash the window and straight in. We got ourselves well geared up with money to get us

clothes and stuff. There was razor gangs at that time but the Beehive weren't, it was mostly stealing. Razors was regarded as below the belt. And we were looked on by the other gangs as being dapper, had a higher standard of living than the usual gangs. We used to go in a tailor's shop in the Gorbals and it cost you five pounds for a real good suit of clothes and the police even accepted us as being on a higher standard, whether they liked it or not, they looked on it that way.

Of course the police wasna fools altogether, young men were going about with new shoes on their feet. The police took the cue there, they says, 'We'll look about for somebody that's well-clad, pick him up.'

They arrested me the first time, they had nothing to go on but they accused me of not having visible means of support. That time I've got on a nice blue suit and well geared up, collar and tie and as I'm walking along a copper tapped me on the shoulder, 'Where are you going laddie? You're looking well today, good suit you've got on, where did you get it? How much money you got in yer pocket?' If you couldn't describe where you got the money that was in yer pocket or the clothes that you're wearing you got a minimum of sixty days' hard labour.

Conditions were so bad inside that every hour counted. I was thrust into what they called the stone yard, that was a quarry, and yer job was to break huge stones into smaller pieces. If you didn't fulfil that then you wouldna get yer remission so you were longer in the jail. All yer hands were blistered because we weren't used to hard work, we were unemployed. There was one particular gang, the Bridgetown Boys, and there were quite a number of these boys in the jail at the same time as me, and they decided that they would strike. They just said they was gonna stop working. To me that wasn't a good idea because I'd only a few days left to go, nevertheless it was riskier for me to refuse to do that because I would maybe get my throat cut so we threw our hammers over the wall and of course I had to do a bit of extra time for that but it was something you just had to accept.

There was one occasion when I threw some bread out the cell window and birds picked it up and ate it, that was good, but of course the warder seen something gettin' thrown out the window so he expected it might be something else, well I was punished severely for that. But you never liked

Larry Rankin, pictured at the age of eighteen, with his mother and sister. Larry was a member of the Beehive Boys, a well-known Glasgow gang involved in crime in the 1920s and 1930s.

Larry Rankin photographed in 1926. Larry and his friends regularly stole cars and took their girlfriends out for 'joyrides' in the countryside around Glasgow.

anyone to see you down or afraid so you just laughed it off, and that was you served yer time until you got out.

Then all we could do was turn back to crime. I had three or four particular pals that helped me. Well, we looked around and we saw other people going about in lovely cars and we had none, we had to walk anywhere we wanted to go, so we thought what a good idea. Once I could drive, well it was an easy thing for me to pick up cars. You only had to get one key and that was you in. It was an easy thing to link up the wires, three or four minutes and you were away. I could go about then, go out with girls, go to dancing, get clothes, live like the people upstairs, and I was happier that way. But if I coulda got a job, a fair job, I would have accepted that, but that wasna the way.

I was only a boy, the wife was just a girl and her father, of course, he didn't like me at all because he knew what I was. I picked up the cars, took the wife away for runs all over various parts of the west of Scotland. We were living like some of the people upstairs for a short period. We'd pick up a decent car to go around in because we found that we got more respect that way. If you went about with an old car the police was liable to pull you up, with a good car they just nodded their head and helped you on yer way. In these days the police weren't as vigilant as what they are today.

Billy, James and myself was out for a night out one time. It was a lovely car we had so we head for Kilmarnock, we get a coupla pints each and we look around us, nothing to do but we just stopped there at this store, smashed the windows in. It was very foolish but we took away about twenty big wirelesses. We're heading back for Glasgow and we had to stop because the police had a road-block.

We were tried. Well it came my turn, I pleaded not guilty and after a lengthy trial I was found guilty, twelve months in Old Duke Street jail.

But when you get out again, you're in the same position. We were only boys that had no means of support, so we turned to crime again."

ANNIE LAI

Annie was born in London in 1905. She moved into Limehouse in the East End of London at the age of sixteen in 1921. For two years she worked as a prostitute and it was in 1923 that she got to know Yuen Sing Lai, a professional gambler and opium dealer. She went to live with Lai and married him. They were together until 1928 when he was deported for attacking a man with an iron bar. The man had apparently been a rival for Annie's affections. After Lai left the country Annie continued to run his opium business and his punk-apu shop, or Chinese gambling den. In 1930 the police closed the shop down and Annie was then forced back into prostitution in order to support herself and her children. She died in 1991.

"Chinatown was like a village of people, all close. Girls used to come down there from leaving home and they'd always be looked after. Some would end up with a Chinaman and after a time move on. It was just a happy atmosphere. And it seemed a kind of security there for anybody that had left home and that, such as in my case.

When Lai heard I was looking for a place to live he said he would give me a room. I had this big double room, very nice too, very reasonable. We weren't living together but he was giving me money and he would give me little packets. 'Will you take this to number so and so?' It would be a matchbox with a few matches in and the opium underneath. I didn't know at the time.

There was a house further up the street where this woman called Nellie lived. She was always in a trance, never awake and her street door was always open. She never got caught so I used to go up there from time to time and have a look at them smoking the opium, that's how I found out how to do it. Of course you must have all the utensils and the bowl and everything. And you have to lay down to it, there's a lamp, see, put it over and the thing bubbles. Some of them used to take such a long, long breath I thought they was never going to start breathing again.

I said to Lai once, 'Lai,' I said, 'have you got some opium, I want to smoke.' 'No!' he went. But I said I wanted it and if he didn't give it me I'd go to Nellie's or somewhere else. So eventually he said, 'All right.' And then up pops everything, the opium and the opium pipe. The first time I did it I felt a bit sick after and so Lai just used to give me a certain amount every day, he saw that I didn't overdo it. And after I became a smoker he used to have these people home to smoke, see.

In the room we took the mattresses off and put boards on, planks of wood. Then you put a blanket to cover it up, a couple of pillows and that and you'd lay all the utensils there in the centre of the bed. They used to hand it all round, it was just like a custom and there used to be a lot of smoke. If you was all aches and pains, bad nerves and that, if you smoke you relax. So long as you don't overdo it you're all right. You had a lovely relaxed feeling and that. I was addicted to it because every so often I used to be all worked-up and in a terrible state.

Then he taught me how to prepare opium, how to get it. I used to go with him and he used to get it over the walls of the docks. Course it's one solid lump and you have to cook it, it takes a long time to cook and you must know how, till it becomes like a thick treacle, like molasses, black and that. The smell is like burning beetroots. And it used to be two shillings a packet.

After a time we got together, sleeping and that. I wouldn't say I was in love with him but I was happy, very happy with him. He was a tall man and people used to look up to him and be kind of scared of him. Every time he used to get in trouble and that, I went to court. Then he got deported and I was on me own. But I still had opium, I still had the pipes and that. So I was having people in my place, always people that you knew, Chinese people, because you'd be afraid to take anybody else and that. I knew the men that had been around when Lai was there and so I got the opium, smuggled it in, prepared it, sold it. I always trusted a Chinaman, they were not hard, they wasn't sexy or wanting different things. They would always look after the women. I lived over a massive big shop, upstairs. So we was more secluded and more safer than other houses although we had a roof outside so anyone could have climbed up. There used to be raids still of course but usually the local bobbies would come to tell me, give them a backhander you know."

GEORGE KIRBY

George and his five sisters were brought up in Toxteth in Liverpool where he was born in 1922. Their father was a gig boatman on the docks. Shortly after leaving school at the age of thirteen, George was caught stealing and sent to a remand home in Newton-le-Willows, Liverpool Farm School. George spent the next few years in and out of reformatories, training-ships and borstal. In December 1939 he joined the Merchant Navy and travelled the world during the Second World War. In May 1942 he was commended for saving a sailor's life after the man fell overboard.

After leaving the Navy George continued his housebreaking and petty crime, spending much of his life in prisons all over Britain until his last 'stretch' ended in 1979. Determined to 'go straight' he got a job as a sales representative. George now lives in London where he sells The Big Issue *newspaper. He has written poems and short stories, many of which have been published. Although George never married he has a son who lives in Liverpool.*

"The first job I got when I left school was a baker's errand boy. On one occasion the shop was empty and I had to go round the back and put the bread there. It was then I helped myself to a couple of bars of chocolate and I began to make a habit of this and then one day I took some money as well, I think about three or four half-crowns. And that's how it all began. Of course I got found out and I went to court and I was placed on probation.

My house was a very poor home. My mum and dad always seemed to be arguing about one thing or another. On one occasion it was definitely money because my father, in a fit of temper, threw a fistful of coins at my mother from the street below.

Some of my pals I went to school with, I used to be invited round there for tea and they had lovely homes and I felt inferior. Why couldn't we have a sideboard and nice carpets? And my mother used to say, 'They've got nice money'. For quite a considerable time I used to have strong feelings, almost bordering on hatred, of my mother. But then I loved my mum, I loved my dad. But I was always trying to sort of get up to my schoolfriends' level and if I was to steal money or steal chocolate and I treated them I'd get an invite to their houses and I'd become one of them, sort of thing.

When I was about thirteen, I broke into the cricket pavilion on Lord Derby's estate, which is on the outskirts of Liverpool. And for that I was actually put away, sent to an approved school, that was the first time I'd been away from home actually.

They sent me to Newton-le-Willows, Liverpool Farm School, a red-brick building, like a stable courtyard, buildings on four sides. When I arrived I went before the governor. He told me what the place was all about, must do as I was told, I'd soon get into the routine and if I behaved myself I would get on very well. He said there was a farm there and was I interested in animals, and I said I liked dogs. He said, 'Oh, we have cows and pigs and hens.'

Well, I was a city boy and I was beginning to miss my mum and dad and I felt, you know, isolated, beginning to pine, getting homesick. I didn't like this set-up at all, having to get up at six o'clock in the morning, go down in the ablution place and brush my teeth together with dozens of other boys. And people pushed you at the side, 'You're a new boy aren't you?' I felt absolutely out of it all you know.

I made up my mind to go, escape. The place wasn't walled in so the opportunity was there. And I just ran, without realizing where I was running to. They came round looking for me in cars and they caught me. I'd only got a short distance and back I went.

Well, I liked it even less when, after I was caught, I was thrashed and they cut all me hair off. I felt utterly humiliated and cried all night. I was being teased and humiliated and spat on more or less by some of the other boys and I

Young offenders pictured at a borstal in Usk in 1945. Inmates of such institutions were subject to a highly disciplined regime, spending long hours carrying out tedious manual tasks.

was determined that the next chance I got I'd go again. And so eventually, after pretending or kidding everyone that I'd settled down, was accepting being there, I just waited and one night I crept through the dormitory window and I was away like a hare.

I was caught again by a policeman this time, and when I was in the police station being detained prior to being taken back, I pulled down me trousers and showed 'em what they'd done to me at the school. My backside was actually cut in three or four places, they'd actually cut the skin when they'd thrashed me. And I grabbed a bottle of ink and said I'd kill meself rather than go back there. I drank the bottle of ink but they just laughed because it was only coloured chalk apparently, they just laughed.

They took me back but that time I just waited until night and then I crept through one of the windows and when I reached the ground I run like hell and kept running for about four or five miles without stopping. I ended up breathless on the railway line under a bridge and I remember sitting there feeling absolutely sorry for myself and saying a little prayer, 'Please God help me get away'.

I didn't know where I was going to, I hadn't got a clue, I knew I daren't go home so I nicked a bike and just kept riding. I remember riding along the coast road in North Wales. And I thought, 'Well, if I hit the wrong way I might go back in a circle.' So I began to call at phone boxes because in them days the phone box had a map and little dots showed you the rough locations of the towns and by that I found me way along the North Wales coast.

Of course, I had to sleep rough, anywhere which was shelter from the wind or the rain. I actually slept in a vacant castle somewhere in North Wales, built like a baronial hall, and built into the floor was a huge table, about thirty foot long. It was a big empty place and I explored all around it that night. And off in the morning again, across Wales. There were times when I was really hungry but the only way I could get any food was to steal it. Sometimes I'd even break into a house. I'd look for an insecure window and creep stealthily in. It was the only way I could survive, 'cos I was a fugitive.

Anyway, I'd gone miles on this bike before they caught up with me. A couple of police in a car stopped me, said they suspected me of being, you know, out of the ordinary, a stranger and that was that, I was caught again.

They put me into a remand home until the masters, the ones who'd thrashed me, could come to take me back to Liverpool. I think it would have been wiser not to have told me this 'cos it made me even more determined not to be taken back. There was about twelve- to fifteen-foot chicken-wire fence around this remand home and that's where we exercised, they let us out there. Well, the first chance I got, soon as the master turned his back, I was up that wire like a lizard and over and away.

I hid low that night, then I started moving, walking or hitching lifts when I could. I ended up in Cirencester, place I'd never heard of before, and there was a huge construction site going on. So I got a job, carpenter's mate. Now I'd be able to have money and spend it legitimately sort of thing. I wouldn't have to go thieving for money. I could buy food. It was there that I learnt how to drive a car, I learnt on the dumper. I had in mind the next vehicle I'd pinch, it wouldn't be a bike, it would be a car.

When the job ended I was on me merry way again and I made my way into London. I had to sleep in a doss-house there which was quite an experience. Jubilee Chambers, the place was full of old men, very primitive, old hospital blankets. I was there for several nights and that was my mistake. Being so young they must have suspected me and I was reported and arrested again.

That was when I was taken to Stamford House Remand Home. They'd given up by then, apparently, wanting to send me back to Newton-le-Willows after my escapades. They said I was not old enough to be sent to borstal and I don't think they knew what to do with me. Then I expressed a desire to go away to sea. I'd heard there was Navy training-ships and much to my pleasure they agreed to send me to one of these ships.

They put me on the RTS *Cornwall* on the Thames, down at Gravesend. I was really happy at the prospect, it was in me thoughts to be a sailor. I wanted to see foreign lands, all the dreams that young people think about but it was a different set-up altogether.

I soon realized it wasn't all that it appeared to be. It was run on the same lines as the navy. As a new boy I sat at the very end of the dining-table. As you progressed, the longer you were there, you got moved up the table. I got my dinner in two tea cups, a potato in one cup and some gravy or soup in the other. If you didn't like it you were told to shut up and this apparently was the way things were.

It was a cruel place, a cruel inhumane place, degrading. When we had a bath you had a master there with a big cane. You'd get into the bath, wash yourself down then he'd smack you on the buttocks. Out you get, next one in and when you're about fourth or fifth through there was about an inch of scum on the water.

There was bullying, and I wasn't a very big boy. There was homosexual advances made to you from the other boys especially if you were new, you were intimidated in more ways than one. If you didn't smoke someone'd come along to ya and put a cigarette down yer jumper and say, 'Right, I want yer ship's pay on Friday'. Ship's pay was two pence.

One bloke, a huge fella, he worked in the kitchens and as I say you were half-fed if you were a new boy. Well he was very kind to me. He was giving me huge slices of jam tart and this was a luxury then and I was very pleased. I didn't

Boys from a reformatory
training ship on a rowing
exercise in 1905.

understand his motives but one day I did when I went to the galley. He walks up and says, 'Come in 'ere a minute'. He dragged me in and tried to take me trousers down. It frightened me, you know.

And if you broke a rule, disobeyed orders in any way, well, the routine was, you knew what to expect. You go to the commander's office and you'd be told, 'Right, you'll be punished at so many hundred hours'. It was quite a ritual, you were taken on to the main deck and all the ship's company lined up. And the captain would stand there literally like Captain Bligh and he would be taking snuff. You bent down and put yer head between the bosun's legs and he held your head like and then your trousers were pulled tight, taut so as to make no gap between yer trousers and yer bare skin. It was usually eight or ten whacks and the captain would count them, 'One, two'. Quite methodical while he was taking his snuff.

I, just like everyone else, I wanted to be a man. I didn't want to scream out. You're given your cap to put in between yer teeth so you can bite on it, 'cos most of us deep down, don't matter how cowardly we may feel, we don't want to look cowardly and so we stifle any desire, temptation to 'Ow'. You bear it the best you can then walk away stinging like hell but trying to keep as brave a face as possible. We want someone to rub our poor wounds but you just can't do that. You have to be brave in front of the others. You feel utterly miserable, as though no one cares, very, very sorry for yourself, humiliated.

I tried to fight it, persevere, tolerate it. You had to fight or go under. I wasn't a coward but, you know, it was too much for me. I couldn't handle it, it was dog eat dog, you had to fend for yourself. True, I learnt all the things I would be required to learn as a sailor and, sadly, some of the things I didn't need to know.

Anyway after about fourteen months I decided I'd had enough of this and I began to get itchy feet – I wanted to escape and I set my plan. Because the ship was anchored out in the middle of the Thames I knew that I needed to swim to the shore and I also knew all about the currents and how you could be swept away and drowned. They'd taught us all that.

Well, all rivers ebb and flow and at the end of the ebb the river stops and begins to turn round. That's called slew tide, that's when there are no fast currents, so I decided that I would swim across at slew tide. There was another lad who wanted to come with me so we came down on the gangway about two o'clock in the morning. It was November and so it was absolutely freezing cold and I swam at the height of slew tide, across to the dredger, took the little boat off the back, clambered up the rudder. I was naked of course and all the barnacles skinned me thigh but you don't feel when you're so excited, you don't feel the cold and the discomfort. I rowed back to the ship for me pal, he had me clothes in a bundle. He threw the bundle in the back, jumped in and off we went. By now the tide had gathered momentum and we ended up in the mud about a mile further down than we intended, but we struggled off through the mud and got dressed.

We had a little argument about which way shall we go. I said, 'I'm going this way.' And he went the other way. I don't know to this day what happened to him.

So I was on the run again and I knew that I had to keep really low so I just had to live by stealing what I could, food, clothes. I became really adept at breaking into houses. It's an animal instinct. I used to want to be sick, you know, nerves must have been tensed up. The first thing I did when I broke into anyone's house was to prepare my escape. I used to open the back door and prop it open with coats so that I could dive through in case I heard just a whisper. If I made any noise they might catch me and if they caught me I'd be sent back to that ship. I've actually broken into houses and I've stepped over a sleeping dog. On one occasion I crawled over a pile of dishes. I'd hear a pin drop 'cos when I went into someone's house I was more frightened than them. I could hear the click of a light switch go on in the bedroom. They were frightened although little did they know I wouldn't harm a fly. And I very seldom ever entered bedrooms. You're just pushing yer luck too far then. I just wanted to get away with it.

Later on I became more expert, stealing money, every penny I could get me hand on, lighters, watches, all the things that could be resold. And you invariably sold them at a loss, all I wanted was the money.

After about a year of living like this, staying at friends', not daring to go home, I broke into this pub. I drank some port wine and it tasted good. I'd never drank before and I pinched some crisps and some cigarettes. As a result of drinking the port wine I think, I got a little bit tipsy and I was a bit careless.

I had a letter with me with an address on in me pocket. I dropped it in this pub as I broke in so the police traced me through that…

They said I was likely to go to prison. Well, it was like a big adventure at first. Maybe I'd seen too many films. I was remanded in Walton Jail. And when I got there it really was completely, you know, horrifying, this was prison.

I was put in a cell, for the first time ever to be in a prison cell. It's only when the screw locks the door and you hear his footsteps walk away that it dawns on you where you are, what it means, you know, no one to talk to, nothing to do. Just walk up and down and in those days it was only one prisoner to a cell. The loneliness, the bare walls. And when you wake up, that's the time I used to feel very sad, very melancholy, when I woke up in the morning and realized where I was, and you hear the doors being unlocked and the harsh voice of screws. 'Rise and shine'.

The first thing was to slop out. You'd take yer pot along the landing where there was a huge sink sluice and you'd pour the contents out, put it under the tap and swill it round. Try and get that over as quickly as possible. Then you'd get yer pint of porridge and yer cup of unsweetened tea, six ounces of bread. You were sent to the mail-bag shop to sew mail-bags and then you got an hour exercise half-way through the morning, where you walked round the exercise yard in single file. You literally weren't allowed to talk to the man in front of you or the man behind. You'd go back to your cell, usually about four o'clock and you were locked up, you were given yer tea, in a cylindrical tin about six inches high, the top lid was like a dish and you'd get the main dish in the big tin and maybe a bit of treacle pudding or rice pudding in the top tin. You'd see on yer cell wall a notice of the menu for 28 days and how many ounces you got. And then you'd be banged up for the night.

It was humiliating by the very clothes you had to wear. They put a little badge on the lapel which stated what part of the prison I was located. I felt like some sort of exhibit. In those days you wore brown, rather coarse brown, ill-fitting. I mean the lapels were cockeyed and the shirts were the same, either too big or too small. It all seemed as if they were made way back in the dark ages, very primitive. And it made you feel inferior, well it was like wearing sackcloth and ashes sort of thing, reminded you of who you were and how far you'd fallen down.

When my remand was over I was packed off to Feltham Borstal. I was given a rough run-down of what the place was all about, the same old lecture you get from anywhere. It seemed to me as though it was being run on the lines of a public school, we had housemasters. I'd been allocated into North House. There was plenty of sporting activity, running, football. I remember I was a swimmer there, I was in the swimming team.

I'd been at Feltham about two months when one day Mr Bailey, the housemaster of North House, came in with rather a serious expression on his face, getting us all to attention. He announced that he'd just been authorized by the Home Office to inform us that war had broken out and that all boys who had completed six months of their sentence would be released immediately with a view possibly of joining the forces. All hell was let loose, chairs went up and I stood there wondering if I was on the list, 'cos I wasn't sure how long I'd been there. Amidst all this carry on and glee I ran down to one of the masters, 'Please sir, am I on that list, have I...?' And he looked through his list and said, 'Yes'. So I joined in with the rest and threw a few chairs around and that's the way it went.

We'd been released to take part in the war effort. The government had decided young fellows, prisoners, could join the army. It was glad for us, sadly, that another world war was about to begin. We were given a suit of clothes, everything, shoes, braces, the lot, and given a railway travel warrant. I arrived in Liverpool on the Sunday afternoon and I remember my mother running out of the house with consternation on her face. 'You haven't run away again have you?' 'No Mam,' I said, 'they've let me out.'"

BABS BRUNNING

Babs, born in 1923, was brought up in Stepney in the East End of London. Her father died when she was six years old and her mother, an office cleaner, was left to bring up Babs, her two sisters and three brothers alone.

In 1936 Babs started work in a cotton mill in Aldgate. She met her future husband, Bob, when he was employed at the local greengrocer's shop which she passed on her way to work. She was fifteen and he was just eighteen. The young couple had their first child, Pat, in 1939 and were married a year later. Babs and Bob now have eight children and still live together in the East End after fifty-four years of marriage.

"Bob used to work in a greengrocer's at the top of our turning, and I'd just left school. I started a job in a cotton factory and as I used to go to work he used to say, 'Good morning'. And I'd get a bit extra. 'A peach for a peach,' he'd say and he'd give me a couple of peaches or something. Then one evening he asked me would I like to go out with him and I said, 'Yes.'

So from then on we went with one another and it was getting a little bit serious. My mother wasn't very pleased about this, in fact none of the family were and after a few months my eldest brother says to me mother, 'I think you should try and break this up a bit, she's too young.' So me mother told Bob to keep away from me.

We were really upset over this and so we had a talk and Bob said, 'Shall we run away together? We'll go to Gretna Green, see if we can get married.' So we ran, packed and went and we only got as far as Walthamstow. We found a room and said we were married to the landlady.

I went out the next day, I got a job, Bob got a job. But when I came home from work the first evening the landlady said to me, 'There's two gentlemen upstairs waiting to see you.' There was two plain-clothes detectives sitting in the room. They questioned me about where Bob was and they even had a photo of him, and then they took me to Stamford House Remand Home.

Course, I cried my eyes out. I had to give all my clothes up and they gave me a basket to put their clothes in, and bathed you, deloused your hair. Then you was given different duties to do like. I had to polish the corridors, down on me hands and knees. They was ever so strict with us, we weren't allowed to talk to the other girls.

I was in there for about a week then I had to come up in front the Juvenile Court. They put me on probation. I kept asking where Bob was but they wouldn't tell me.

I was very, very frightened and I was worried. I cried such a lot you know and wondered what was going to happen. But I was so in love with him and I had it in my mind that nobody was going to stop me from seeing him so this is why I'd got the strength to carry on.

I didn't see him till the court case at the Old Bailey, No 1 Court. I went up there with my mother and my brother and they brought Bob up from the cells and stood him in front of the judge. He looked really shaken. They questioned him and then they called me up as a witness. I had to swear an oath and I started to cry. And then the judge asked me if Bob forced me to go away, did he make me leave home, did he force me to have intercourse? I told them I went of my own free will. Then the judge said to my mother, 'Well,' he said, 'it won't last long, it's just infatuation.'

Bob was given three years probation and he was told to leave my neighbourhood. After that of course we was banned from meeting again but I found out where he was and we made a meet. We just used to see each other in secret.

It wasn't long till they found out that I was pregnant. The probation officer found me a place in City Road Hospital, a maternity hospital, and I had to work in the kitchen there from eight o'clock in the morning till nine o'clock at night until the baby was due to be born. I used to have Sunday evenings off and Bob used to come round the side and I used to sneak out and meet him, go for a walk, and he used to see me back to the hospital and that was it. We used to sit and talk about things and we just used to say, 'Well, we'll carry on, we'll carry on till they let us get married.' Carry on till I was old enough to get married. I used to cry.

I used to say to me mother, 'Why don't you let me see him? I love him.' She said he was no good for me and that I had to have the baby adopted. All the time in the hospital they sort of pressured me, 'Why don't you have the baby adopted?'

But I stuck to what me and Bob had said all along and when the baby was twelve months old my mother finally gave in and let us get married. So we had a quiet wedding and that was it, we've been together ever since."

SPUD MURPHY

Spud was born in 1926 in Deptford, south-east London. His mother died when he was eleven months old and his father, an Irish labourer, placed Spud in an orphanage in Sidcup. After six years his grandmother took him in to live with her in Deptford, using him to chop wood and do many other heavy chores for her. Spud ran away at the age of thirteen and found work with the local 'totters' or rag-and-bone men, sleeping at night in their stables.

Spud began to steal to survive and in 1942 he was caught and sentenced to two years at North Sea Camp Borstal in Boston, Lincolnshire. He spent the next five years of his life in the army, much of the time in military prisons for desertion.

In 1949 Spud married and got a job with the Central Electricity Authority. It wasn't until the breakdown of his marriage in 1956 that he returned to crime and was sent to prison for eighteen months for breaking and entering. Spud remarried in 1982. He now has six children and still lives in Deptford.

"I just ran away to live on me own and when you're in a situation without any discipline you become wild. I became rebellious, I didn't like authority. I owed the world nothing, I owed society nothing and they gave me nothing. Feelings didn't come into it, it was just living the only way I knew.

I used to go out rag-and-boning and they might buy me a cup of tea and a sandwich. Work hard all day and in the evening they might take me in an' 'ave another cup of tea and a sandwich and give me, say, two shillings. With that two shillings I had enough for another cup of tea, go to the pictures, buy five cigarettes and live like a king for two hours. Then I used to come out of the warmth of the pictures and come back to reality to go back to sleep in the rag-'n-bone man's stables.

Sleeping in the stables was shelter but at the same time it made me very envious when I used to try and walk round the streets late at night to tire myself out and I seen ordinary children with families living in a house, love and care, and the only companion I had was the 'orse and the dog. I just used to sleep on the straw. The rag-and-bone man had overcoats to put on when it was raining, I'd just take one of them and cover meself over. It was cold, bitter cold, and I just become immune to it, it was just try and get to sleep. The rats would be gnawing or dogs barking and horses kicking their hooves but you just got used to it.

I couldn't go with a rag-and-bone man to work on a Saturday or a Sunday so I had no payment to survive then, I had to steal, Hobson's choice. It becomes compulsive because when you first start you don't get caught, you want to go on to bigger things. Before you know where you are you're in the fourth division of stealing. Anything that was an easy catch I was there like a fisherman to get it to survive. My conscience never pricked me at all. As long as I knew it was going to get me through that day. At the age of thirteen you're not an educated person like in stealing, so you might steal something that's worth say five pounds and sell it for a ridiculous thing of a pound, but that pound was for food next day and surviving.

I've stole women's purses, you know follow a woman, when she puts her bag down to pick the shopping up I would either have the bag or the purse and away. I would never use like violence, do it crafty, jump on the back of a horse and cart like, to get away. If you call violence using me fists I've 'it someone but I've never used an object or maimed anyone. Might have head butted 'em or just hit 'em with me fist. Stealing by wits that's all.

I got chased and I got caught but in the area where I lived most people knew me and knew me circumstances and nine times out of ten I'd get a good clump round the ear or a kick up the backside, no police was involved. It sort

A scene from the 1946 film *Children on Trial*.

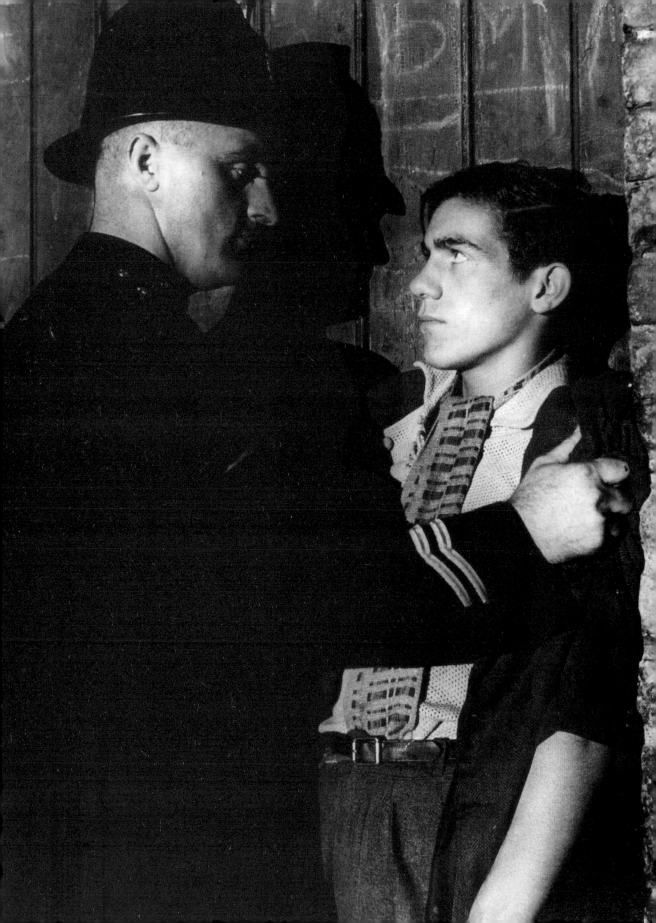

The exercise yard at Usk Borstal in 1945. An important part of the regimented daily routine in these institutions was military drill.

of give me a licence to carry on, just get a punch in the ear and something. The police, they used to have little coins in their gloves and sometimes they'd give you a good slap round the ear with it, but there would come a time when their patience was pushed too much and then they would take us to the police station, more or less to frighten you.

I started off on meself but then when you gotta sell something you gotta find someone else who's willing to buy it. So someone might say, 'We know somewhere where it's a bit big, we need four of us.' And that's how you first start to get involved in like a gang. 'Oh that Spud ain't a bad bloke at stealing.' Then some other gang wants you to go with them and it snowballs.

Crime then was quite easy. Most of the police was in the armed forces and so there was only a skeleton-like police force. There was reserve policemen but after they'd done a day's work and they went out on a night-time they was knackered anyway. To me they was only Mickey Mouse policemen, just used to laugh and tell 'em to fuck off. They'd think twice about approaching ya. And what did they have? A little whistle to blow, time they blew the fuckin' whistle you'd be up the M1 somewhere.

When people was down in the air-raid shelters, their 'ouse was at risk to most people. The first thing you used to do was wait until you heard an aeroplane overhead and then you'd hear an air raid siren warning you know, and you would look for an 'ouse. It'd be completely blacked-out and don't forget there was no street lighting, everything was in darkness so that was to your advantage. You knew ninety-nine per cent of the people was running down the air-raid shelters and most of the brothers, the sons, the husbands, they was away in the army so you knew in the household there was only like a woman or sisters or the grannies and all that, so you knew you had a licence to practically go in any house. And people didn't used to bother about locking their doors, they knew they might get blown to pieces by a bomb so it's nine out of ten we could just open the doors. You looked for ration books and identity cards because you could sell 'em for a lot of money. Or a publican might shut his pub you know and run down the shelter and you'd break a window and get in and take any cigarettes in there or a bottle of whisky and sell it.

You come out in the morning, streets upon streets of 'ouses was flattened and where some people had jewellery left indoors and money or something like that we just used to look for it. That was looting really. But there wasn't a lot of police about so you could do it with impunity. That's what I had to do.

You could sell more or less anything on the black market, easy. And lorry loads like of meats, soap or anything, you just went after 'em. You come across a load of cigarettes and you had a fortune. To steal a lorry load of stuff you followed it and got talkin' to the driver, might be in the pub and say, 'Cor, I saw you driving a lorry today.' 'Yeah, I had to go in the docks and get a load of sugar.' And you'd go on from there and very likely he might go in a café later and then you jump in the lorry and drive it away.

Or sometimes the lorries used to have to go and unload and we just used to wait and sometimes we'd get the pox of waiting, we'd just jump in the first motor and take it, don't matter what. Come unstuck one day, we stole a lorry load of stuff and I thought to myself, 'We've really got it made today'. We took it round to go and sell it at the slaughterhouse, where you dispose of stolen goods. When we opened the back up it was full of dolls' eyes.

Principles was never to use violence, never to hold people, try not to take it off of people who was worse off than yourself. If someone could afford it they was the targets.

I'd faced up to so much in life it didn't bother me about getting caught. But when I was sixteen I got sent to borstal. I spent six months on remand in Brixton, then I got three years borstal.

It was hard work there 'cos they humiliated you. You had to wear short trousers, ankle socks, treated like a little boy dress-wise but work-wise they treated you as a man, reclaiming land from the sea in the north, up to yer waist in mud in the winter and the wind and the snow and the blow. And the rebel in me said, 'No, I'm not gonna do it.' And if you didn't do it you was sent away for punishment, bread and water. Well, I had bread and water instead of the howlin' winds and the salt getting into me chapped legs, a luxury really.

But there were other ways they could get you. I've been taken into the bathroom by three or four officers, given a good beating just because I told one of the prison officers to go and fuck himself. I said, 'You're only a prison officer because you haven't got the brains to be a policeman and you haven't got the guts to be a thief.' And then they'd put things like all cow shit in yer shoes and then time you cleaned them out and cleaned yerself up the fuckin' meals was over and you was hungry. I've known 'em spit on yer food and if you're hungry you eat it. They spit on me chips once and I said, 'Why don't you piss on 'em? We ain't got no vinegar.'

They'd use every trick in the book to get at you and you couldn't do nothing. I mean, if you got a beating in front of ten other officers they'd say they didn't see nothing. You got black eyes, you got cuts, you got cracked ribs. But I was hardened to it and it upset them not me, because they couldn't upset me. I could suffer physical pains but what they tried to do to me emotionally couldn't 'urt me no way 'cos emotionally then I didn't have a lot of feelings.

There was no point in escaping, you was thirty miles from anywhere, isolated. If you reached the end of the thirty mile they'd only be there waiting for ya with a severe good beating.

'Cos of the war and that they let me out to get me in the army. Well, I didn't want to be patriotic, I didn't really want to fight in no wars. Society owed me nothing and I owed society nothing. I had to struggle to reach a certain age and when I reached that certain age why should they take the cream of my life? They didn't worry about me so why should I be involved in the propaganda and go and kill people and get killed? I was a sort of a rebel.

I thought borstal was bad enough but when I got in the forces I never met such a lot of bastards in all my life. 'Stand to attention, to do this, double up 'ere, double up there.' They tried to put a uniform on me and I wouldn't have it and they forced it on me and I just deserted, ran off. I said, 'Aye, fuck this I'm off.' First thing, I got all me equipment, rifle, bayonet and everything and go down the River Thames and throw the fucking lot in, that's what I thought of it. Then I used to go and find casual work in Deptford. The bosses where you worked knew you was a deserter from the army and worked you 'ard all day and you'd line up for yer pay of a night-time and the bastards would phone the police. So eventually you had to revert back to thieving again.

I found a place, a factory near Millwall football ground, used to make glass bottles. Well, underneath there was like a big cellar and it was so warm in the winter where the furnaces were. All the deserters used to get down there and the police didn't used to come to us much because they knew we was strong in numbers. We used to survive down there, thieving, surviving. And always make sure a window was open or something so you could jump out the back.

But I mean I've been amongst the debris digging people out, dying and injured and crippled and blood all over the place. I 'elped in New Cross when the rocket dropped and three hundred and sixty people got killed. Not digging for hours, I'm talking about days digging to help people out. The deserters went

Boys doing building work at North Sea Camp Borstal during the war. Spud Murphy was sentenced to three years at this camp in 1942.

out then, don't matter they were gonna get captured, they still done it so we did have a lot of good principles as well as bad.

And then if you did get caught stealing you got put back in prison. Then when you come out of prison you 'ad the army waiting for you and then they charge you with desertion. You'd be back in prison, in the army prison, shave all your hair off and half starve ya and run the bollocks off ya and then, when they let you out, expect you to be a good soldier so you just fucked off again. A vicious circle, never-ending.

They used to have jeeps running about the streets with about four military police in and one day they took me unawares. I got caught, they took me to Woolwich barracks, handcuffed me and said, 'You're a fucking deserter and fucking good men's getting killed. You're going to have a court martial.'

They said, 'You gotta put an army uniform on.' 'No,' I said, 'not me.' So they stripped me off completely naked and about five of 'em held me on the cell floor and they said, 'Oh, he needs a shave.' They just got a razor and I had about four days growth on me chin and they just got a dry razor and ripped it off of me. Then they just forced the uniform on me but as soon as they got it on me I stripped it off again, took the fucking lot off.

The night before I was gonna have me court martial they said, 'You'll get a hundred and twelve days in prison, army imprisonment.' They took me out the cell and into this office where I was gonna have me court martial and told me to clean it up. So just to get out the cell for a while I didn't mind cleaning it up and I had to put a big Union Jack on the table where the officers were going to sit. And so I shit right in the middle of it. Next morning they knew it was me that done it and I got me hundred and twelve days so I just turns round and says, 'Bollocks to the lot of you.'"

2

A DANGEROUS PASSION

AFFAIRS

On Sunday 25 November 1928 the *News of the World* featured a front-page 'special' under the headline CURTAIN FALLS ON INTRIGUE: SHOOTING OF A NURSE AND MARRIED MAN:

"Tomorrow the coroner for south-east London will investigate the circumstances of, and seek the motive for, a remarkable double tragedy in his district yesterday afternoon. Behind the locked door of a good-class home in Peckham Rye, a married man and a pretty hospital nurse passed to swift and silent death from revolver bullets through the brain.

They had been firm, fast friends for many months secure in their intrigue by the knowledge that the breadth of the metropolis lay between the married man's home and their nightly meeting place. That they were on exceedingly affectionate terms was common knowledge amongst the nurse's colleagues, but, on the other hand, friends and acquaintances of the man were amazed to learn last night that he had any other 'interest' apart from his work and home.

The dead – or dying – couple were discovered in dramatic fashion by a policeman, to whom the front-door key had been thrown from an upstairs window. Five minutes later the victims were carried out to an ambulance, the nurse still in the uniform of her calling. Hours passed before identity became definite, but the police were satisfied eventually that the victims were: Miss Winifred Rumble, 25, a tall, dark and good-looking nurse, who had a room on the third floor back; and Gerald Theodore Hartnell, 35, a married man of Redcots, Heming Road, Edgware."

The tragedy and melodrama of affairs that went wrong – especially if they involved suicide pacts – were front-page news in the Sunday scandal sheets of the 1920s and 1930s. The reports were highly sensational, and no doubt distorted, yet they provide one of the few records of what was then roundly condemned as adultery or infidelity. For the taboos surrounding sex outside marriage were so strong they ensured that very little of this extra-marital activity ever came into public view. The church, which wielded far greater power than it does today, preached that adultery was a cardinal sin. Sexual respectability was considered very important in many office jobs like banking and insurance and if there was a whiff of scandal, a married man or woman's career prospects could be ruined. Lord Reith would not even allow anyone who was divorced to work for the BBC. In this atmosphere most affairs remained very secret, known only to the few people who were directly involved or affected by them.

It was generally assumed that affairs were on the increase during the first decades of the twentieth century. Commentators pointed to the rise in the divorce rate as their main evidence. In the 1900s there were only about 500 divorces a year in a married population of around 11 million. By the late 1930s the annual divorce rate had increased to around 7500. This was still extraordinarily low compared with today (where one in every three marriages ends in divorce), with less than one in every 2000 marriages ending in divorce. But these figures are very unreliable as an indicator of the extent of extra-marital affairs which were undoubtedly far more widespread than a head count of divorces on the grounds of adultery might suggest. Very few cases of adultery ended in divorce because of the stigma attached to broken marriages and to the cost and complexity of divorce proceedings. In the absence of proper legal aid divorce was to a large extent a privilege of the well-to-do. And even they could fall victim to the continuing moral shame of divorce, as was vividly illustrated in 1936 with the abdication of Edward VIII over his proposed marriage to the American divorcee Mrs Simpson.

Most of the explanations offered at the time for the supposed increase in affairs pointed to the instinctive male desire for sexual adventure and to the double standard which excused in men sexual conduct that was forbidden for women. As sex researchers Buschke and Jacobsohn put it in their *Introduction to*

A couple photographed walking out on a Bank Holiday in 1904. In the early years of the century there were only about five hundred divorces per year in a married population of approximately eleven million.

A 1930s depiction of the jealous wife finding a photograph of her husband's mistress. The double standard of the time assumed that whilst wives stayed at home looking after the children their husbands could seek sexual pleasure elsewhere.

Sexual Hygiene (published in 1932), 'Men, being more polygamously inclined than women have claimed for themselves the right to change their sexual partners whenever the fancy takes them and the opportunity arises.' Traditionally, married men had found discreet sexual pleasure with prostitutes or mistresses while their wives were occupied at home with the children. Most notoriously in the outposts of the British Empire far from home, there were considerable opportunities for sexual misconduct amongst civil servants and army officers, leading to recurrent scandals. By the 1930s, however, prostitution was in rapid decline both in the colonies and in Britain. Many commentators believed this was a consequence not of higher moral standards but of increasing numbers of married men deriving their sexual pleasures from affairs.

The emergence of the 'modern woman' was widely blamed in the 1920s and 1930s for this increase in sexual opportunities open to married men. Young women were beginning to enjoy more personal freedom and independence, rejecting old-fashioned notions of domesticity and dutiful obedience to elders and betters. The archetypal modern woman smoked, wore make-up, danced to jazz and worked alongside men in offices, which had until recently been male preserves. She also had higher expectations of romance and sexual fulfilment in marriage than did previous generations. *Ideal Marriage*, a sex guide for married couples written by Theodore Van de Velde, which offered advice on how husbands and wives could achieve mutual orgasms, became a bestseller in the 1930s. One sign that sexual relationships were becoming increasingly important in marriage was documented by the Divorce Law Reform Union. Most of the 20 000 letters it received from those wishing to end their marriages complained of sexual distaste or dissatisfaction with their partners.

All this was extremely shocking to a large section of British society who saw these changes as a grave threat to the stability of marriage and family life. The Social Purity and Hygiene Movement, backed by the churches, campaigned to warn people of the dangers of sexual freedom and adultery. Propaganda films like *Whatsoever A Man Soweth* (1919), *John Smith and Son* (1932) and *Trial for Marriage* (1936), showed infidelity and affairs leading inevitably to the horror of venereal disease, for which there was no effective cure.

While it would be misleading to exaggerate the freedom of the modern woman, there were fundamental social changes in the first decades of the century – at home, at work and in leisure time – the effect of which was to give women (and men) more opportunities to form sexual liaisons outside marriage. One of the most important was the more effective use of birth control methods by married men and women. This reduced the risk of unwanted pregnancy resulting from affairs. It also helped them to control the number of children they had and reduce their family size. By the 1930s more than three-quarters of all families had three or less children. Most married women were no longer worn down by the drudgery of constant childbearing and child rearing. Their husbands too, as a consequence, had fewer family ties and commitments. To those who opposed the increasing emancipation of women, the link between family size, affairs and divorce was absolutely clear. In the 1920s and 1930s around half of all those seeking divorce were childless couples, and around a third were couples with just one child. Figures like these could, of course, be interpreted in a variety of ways, but there was no doubt in the mind of Anthony Ludovici, writing in *Woman: A Vindication* in 1923:

> "Human courtship and the subsequent union of the sexes to which it leads is full of the excitement, the doubt, the anxiety and the final triumph of the huntsman. Beside this however, the steady hum-drum routine of married life can at best only be a flat parody... Children are obviously a source of variety in the home. Each child in its turn, gives the home a different aspect, a different outlook, a different responsibility. Children moreover, give the family unity a superior aim and purpose, which increases in importance with the number of offspring. In this sense alone, therefore, a state of childlessness or of family limitation constitutes a dangerous state from the standpoint of connubial stability... From the statistics it would appear that more women than men go wrong in a childless marriage. This is only what from our argument we should have expected. It is obvious that during the sixth, the seventh, eighth and ninth years of marriage, most couples who are attempting to limit their families will have ceased from procreating. The wife will therefore tend to become increasingly impatient with her lot, and ultimately make a confidant of some idiot of a man, who will interpret her marked attentions as a proof of his irresistible charm and the two will end in what the world is pleased to call 'falling in love'."

A few sex reformers took a more radical view of affairs. Bertrand Russell proposed a reassessment of adultery in the new era of birth control and greater equality between the sexes. He argued that open sexual relationships were healthy and could add interest and variety to married life without undermining its stability. Following this sexual philosophy quickly proved to be disastrous for Russell's own marriage which disintegrated after his wife Dora fell in love with the journalist Griffin Barry and had his baby. Nevertheless open relationships became fashionable for a time amongst a small artistic and literary set. Gay and lesbian affairs though were, for the most part, still too taboo to be discussed openly. Those who had homosexual affairs – like the writer Vita Sackville-West – usually chose to keep them secret. The writer, Radclyffe Hall, however, made no attempt to disguise her sexual orientation. She had an open affair with Una Tronbridge, the wife of an admiral. Her novel, *The Well of Loneliness* (1928), which sought to portray the predicament of lesbians in a homophobic society, was prosecuted for obscenity. It became an immediate bestseller.

It took the disruption of the Second World War finally to shatter the myth of sexual respectability that had for so long surrounded married life in Britain. In the 'last dance' atmosphere of 1939 and 1940 there was a marriage boom in which about 22 people in every 1000 got married. Three out of every ten brides were under twenty-one. Many barely got to know their partners before they were posted overseas for long periods. To begin with most seem to have been faithful but by 1942, the third year of the war, many marriages had foundered. Husbands formed close relationships with local women or women serving alongside them in the armed forces. And intimate barrack-room relationships between men led some to discover a new homosexual identity.

Married women too began to take advantage of some of the new freedoms the war gave them. Paid work outside the home gave them money to spend and a new circle of friends with whom they could enjoy an occasional 'girls' night out' at the local cinema or dance hall. This could open up new horizons and it was here that many met servicemen not just from all over Britain, but also from many of the Allied countries. The American GIs – oversexed, overpaid and over here – were especially glamorous. As an ordinary GI earned four times the wages of his British counterpart he could be an attractive friend for a wife whose husband was away. In the wartime atmosphere of 'living for the present' friendships often led to affairs – just as they had during the First World War when there was a similar, though smaller scale, pattern of infidelity and marital breakdown.

Most tried to keep their affairs secret. This was much easier for men serving in another country than for women, whose children, relatives, in-laws and neighbours knew their every movement. Those without children sometimes moved away or moved in with a lover, pretending to be his wife, in order to win respectability and escape from the family. Most though had no choice but to remain at home. Their distress was frequently compounded by unwanted pregnancies. The numbers of married women having abortions, according to some official estimates, doubled during the war. So too did the illegitimate birth-rate, rising to a quarter of a million – a third of all births – by 1945. In a rare survey undertaken by Birmingham's Public Health Department it was observed that during the last years of the war around one in three of all the city's illegitimate children were born to married women. Many of these unwanted babies were taken for adoption which increased dramatically during the war.

A few (mostly men), tried to avoid the problems that serious affairs brought in their wake, by simply ignoring the marriage laws altogether. They acquired a second spouse while still legally married to the first. There was a startling rise in prosecutions for bigamy from around 300 a year in the late 1930s to 1135 in 1945.

The divorce rate doubled during the war. But in many cases affairs were kept secret until the war was over. It was only then that many couples, trying to pick up the threads of the relationship with the virtual stranger they were married to, were forced to confront the reality of what had happened during their years apart. Countless numbers decided to forgive and forget, often for the sake of the children. For many others the hurt was too great and they petitioned for divorce. The number of divorces rocketed to what was then the highest ever figure of 60 000 in 1947. Around two-thirds of these immediate post-war divorces were initiated by husbands. The prime cause of these divorces was, on the face of it, the infidelity of the wives. However, it seems likely that this was another example of the double standard. Husbands at the front felt it was their right to visit prostitutes or have affairs, but they expected their wife to remain faithful and 'wait' for them. The high rate of infection with venereal disease in the armed forces – which was around ten times higher than amongst civilians – certainly suggests that many husbands were sexually active while away from home.

One important aim of post-war reconstruction and the early Welfare State was to stabilize marriage and family life after the disruption of the war. At the heart of the new vision was the devoted mother who stayed at home to look after her children. As couples settled down once again to their old gender roles and their domestic routines, so the divorce rate declined, first to 31 000 in 1950, then to a low of 23 000 in 1958. Nevertheless it remained two and a half times higher than it had been before the war. It is far from certain though that this was due to couples having more affairs. The increase was probably due more to the Labour government who in 1948 made legal aid for divorce proceedings available for the majority of the working classes. For the first time divorce was open to the poor too.

One interesting footnote to our research into memories of affairs before the 1950s is that we found it much more difficult to find older people prepared

---

A soldier says goodbye to his family before leaving for France in 1939. Separated from their spouses many husbands and wives began affairs and by the end of the war the divorce rate had doubled.

to talk openly about this subject than any other documented in the book. Many admitted that affairs were commonplace – and sometimes that they had had an affair themselves – but they did not wish to discuss their personal experiences in any detail. This was especially the case with men, none of whom wanted to be quoted. For some the pain, the guilt and the embarrassment of affairs was still uncomfortably fresh in their minds. Others, understandably, did not want their partners or their family to know of affairs that had happened a long time ago and had never been spoken about. Despite the sexual revolution, since the sixties, affairs remain a subject most of those who married during the first half of this century seem to want to keep secret.

MARJORIE HOPKINS

Marjorie was born in Huddersfield in 1909. Her father worked at the cotton mill and she had one brother and four sisters. When she was fourteen Marjorie went into the cotton mill to work as a spinner. In 1930 she married and had three children. Her husband, a millworker, died in 1976. Marjorie now lives alone in Huddersfield.

Left: Marjorie Hopkins photographed with two of her children in the 1930s.
Above: Marjorie Hopkins' husband playing with their children.

"We lived with his mother and I never went out with him. He said, 'It's your place 'ere.' But he were still going out with everybody. He'd come 'ome on Friday, give me me money, some nights he hasn't come 'ome at all, stayed somewhere else.

And he used to batter me, he was very violent, yes, I've had many a good hidin', black marked and all over, all over me, kicked me and all sorts.

Then I 'eard that me husband was going with this woman, Carrie. A woman on street told me, she said, 'We've seen 'em down steps at it.' So I said, 'Well, let him, I'm not bothered.' And then this Carrie had this baby and I actually helped to bring it into the world and I found out when it were about six months old it were his. Me daughter used to fetch this baby on every day to play with it and do like, and one day me husband were at 'ome, he was sitting at table. Our Marian came t'door with that babby and so I just said, 'Marian, take that baby 'ome and don't fetch it n'more, cos yer father there, he's father to that babby.' So she took it 'ome and she never fetched it again. I uptipped table and there were everything on it, breakfast table, pots, sugar and tea. I said, 'Now you can fettle that up and you can clean that up.' He said, 'I'm not.'

I didn't feel anything, nowt about 'im, he were just nothin' to me, nothing. He wasn't there to me, he looked after hisself, made his own meals and the lot. I wouldn't sleep with him. He comes to me for sex and I said, 'Look,' I said, 'get away from me and don't come near me no more.' He said, 'What?' I said, 'Don't come near me no more, that's the finish.'

I went to Carrie though and I says, 'That kid's John's.' She says, 'It isn't.' I says, 'It is, it's just like him, I'll bloody kill ya.' And I chased her. I were that mad I would have killed her, I just gave her another bash, I said, 'Look, you can have him, you can have my 'usband for good, I don't want him. Don't never speak to me no more, nor yer kid.'

But then she, she used to snigger at me every time she saw me. So I told him we had to leave the street. We moved to Manchester Road and we bought this house two pound a week, no interest, no nothin'. I forgot 'er then, that didn't bother me at all. And although he were living with me, I forgot 'im. We never spoke nor nowt. I had three kids by him and I just looked after them. I only stopped because he were all right with kids."

ALISON PIERSON

Alison, born in 1909 in Sutton Coldfield, was educated at boarding school in Harrogate. Her father had been an international hockey player and her mother was a painter. At the age of eighteen Alison left school and began a series of lone travels to Europe and the Middle East. She became a Fellow of the Royal Geographical Society in her early twenties. In 1930 she started to have an affair with an uncle of one of her friends which was to last for several years until she married in 1935 and lived in Baghdad where her husband worked for the Foreign Office. They had three children.

In 1941 Alison's husband arranged for her and their children to be 'evacuated' to India. Alison was to stay in Kashmir as the guest of an army surgeon. During her stay in Kashmir they began an affair and married in 1943 after Alison's divorce. Later that year she gave

Alison Pierson and her three children, in 1941, after they had been
evacuated to India.

*birth to their son and they lived together with the children from her
first marriage.*

    *After the death of her second husband in 1950 Alison ran her
own hotel in Bombay before moving back to settle in England where
she remarried. She is now a widow and lives with her youngest son in
London.*

    "It developed entirely from my first kiss at the age of twenty-one, at my
schoolfriend's twenty-first birthday party, and I just fell in love with him,
Jimmie. He was thirty years older than I was. He had a wife, he had two

children. No question ever of breaking anything up. Although his relationship with his wife was very, very patchy. He used to spend most of his nights at the club, playing bridge, to get home late.

I met him three times a week, perhaps in London. He went to the office, I went to Harrods or whatever I did and we met up again later on. We lunched, we went to the theatre. I was accepted even at the Devonshire Club. I mean they all had their extras you know, these men's clubs, so I just fitted in beautifully. Oh hell, all wealthy professionals had something, you don't really think people were still 'till death us do part' do you? 'Keep thee only unto her.'

We had private dining-rooms at night, which meant of course going to bed as well. We slept naked together, it was anything but platonic but it was never quite right over the mark. I had to remain a virgin and I did, and Jimmie was quite willing. He had whatever he wanted somewhere else I'm sure. I just loved him and he loved me.

I wasn't a paid mistress, let me get that straight absolutely. I was dined and wined but I was never paid, I had no jewellery. I didn't want anything, I was happy. I asked nothing, he demanded nothing, but we did genuinely have enormous affection for each other.

When I left England to start travelling, naturally I left Jimmie behind somewhat although we were always friends, right up to his death. But I met my husband in Baghdad and began to live there. I didn't love him. Simply I wanted to have children and he seemed like a suitable father for them. And I concluded that if I gave him the children he wanted and I wanted, love would be automatic. I was very stupid if you like. I was a baby-making machine, he wanted one and I was willing to be one.

We had the three children who I adored and during the war my husband and I decided for their safety I must take them away from Baghdad for a while. We had a distant connection in India and I knew I could get an introduction there. It was arranged that I should take the children to live with a doctor called Bob in his enormous house in Kashmir.

Kashmir was the most beautiful place in the world and he lived there. He was a Colonel Sahib, do you see? Damned difficult, he couldn't put his own bloody trousers on, he held his legs out and a bearer put them on for him. He got the man out of bed at four o'clock in the morning to take his uniform boots off.

Alison Pierson with her lover pictured at the foot of the Himalayas in 1942. They married a year later.

**Alison Pierson and her second husband at their home in Kashmir
in the late 1940s.**

So I was in that house, living with what I realized at once was the most
wonderful man. I had never even shaken hands with him. I'd met him, yes, and
then he said one night, 'Look here, we'll go to the Maharajah's garden party
tonight.' And I said, 'Oh, no, no, no, I don't want to be seen with you, people
will start talking, I'm living in the house.' And he said, 'Don't be stupid, the
Maharajah's not having a garden party every week.' So we went and it was
there apparently that he made up his mind he wanted me.

I still had never touched him but we got on to the dance floor and I was
electrified, from head to foot and terrified. I knew that husbands, children or

nothing was going to matter, and we got back that night and he said, 'Come and have sandwiches, they're all laid out, and a drink'. But I ran upstairs to bed.

The next day he asked me out to dinner on the lake and again I refused. I was very, very frightened and I didn't want to be unfaithful. I had made a marriage and we had the children. But he told me about the lakes, one of the most beautiful places in the world, and these boats just drifting in and out of the lotus plants and he persuaded me. Well, if you know anything about Kashmir those are the troublemakers, those boats, they are full length, lovely beds, the man with his little oar behind is out of sight, and he kissed me there for the first time. When we got back he said, 'Now, am I coming up to you? Will you go upstairs and get into bed?' And I put my hand on his arm and I said, 'Yes, I will.'

From then onwards everything was all I'd never imagined. I had lived a sort of happy, orderly, sexless, institutional life as a married woman, full of dinner parties, full of tennis, I had a horse and I had everything I wanted, and my children. And now this, the most wonderful love affair.

After some months though I realized I had to go back to face my husband. I told him one evening that I was going to return to Baghdad and we both looked at each other. I crumpled, he crumpled, I've never known a man cry, he blubbed like a schoolboy and this was most gratifying, I can assure you. I mean it, it was for me, and I absolutely adored this man.

But I set out with my children to go back to my husband. I got down to Karachi and lost eleven pounds in eight days. I didn't know what I was doing, I was screaming crackers, I'd never been in love before. My husband met me at the other end and took us back to the house. I just ran upstairs and howled in the bathroom, locked myself in.

I didn't know where to go and for about four months I wouldn't let my husband touch me. He asked me what the hell had gone on in India? But I just told him that I was ill. And he didn't know whether to believe me or not, or what to do until we realized I must go back. He knew he couldn't stop me.

I went back and apparently for all the time I had been away my Bob had never slept properly, he didn't even go to bed. He sat up all night the servants told me. He just used to knock off his boots and his shirt and sit in a chair till four o'clock in the morning. He couldn't go to bed with thinking I was sleeping with my husband. Now, there, you've got somebody who really loved you, hadn't you?"

ODETTE LESLIE

Odette was born in 1924 in Hove but grew up in North London with her father, a caterer, and her mother, a musician. She had one sister and one brother. Odette started work when she was fourteen as a kennel maid. In 1939 she joined the ATS but was thrown out after six months for being under age. She then went to work in a bar in Fleet Street in London where she was also a singer. In 1942 she married her husband a week after they had met and he was posted overseas just months after the wedding. Odette was called up to do war work in a Spitfire factory. In 1949 she divorced her husband and remarried later that year in Jersey. She has one son, born in 1950. Odette now lives in Morecambe.

"A lot of young people got married on the spur of the moment during the war. You don't know from one minute to the next what's going to happen, whether he's going to be sent away, whether a bomb is going to hit. I'd only known my husband briefly and then a week later we were married. We were strangers going into a situation of marriage. It was just romantic, we are going to be married, we will be a pair, he will come back, we will have children, we will have a cottage, we'll have roses round the door. But it didn't have any basis. He was back to barracks the next day but on the wedding night I actually did get pregnant.

We didn't have our own place so I was living with my mother. Anyway on his next leave the atmosphere was awful and I couldn't figure out why, and only on the very last night of his leave he told me it was an embarkation leave. I was shattered because I didn't expect him to go abroad so soon. He'd volunteered. I didn't see him again for three years.

Then I was very unlucky and lost the baby. It was shattering, I got very bitter and couldn't handle it. I was working sixty hours a week in a war factory making petrol tanks for Spitfires, so the strain was physically terribly taxing. Along with this, night after night we were bombarded by the raids.

You were desperate for some sort of outlet, something to help you through the day. I was a young woman, and because I'd been married, however briefly, I was sexually aware, awakened to things. I was just vulnerable and open for something to happen.

It happened to me in 1943. I used to go to a little club, singing there. Anyway one night there was a new drummer, very slim, very attractive young man, very good drummer. I suppose I was almost waiting for it to happen and the chemistry was immediate. He was attracted to me, I was certainly attracted to him. I didn't feel any guilt or feel it was wrong because I'd been married so briefly and my husband was three thousand, six thousand miles away, he didn't exist, he wasn't real. All he was was the odd air letter every three months. I wore a wedding ring but I didn't feel married.

This Hughie, the drummer, he was about ten years older than me, and we started a relationship. I actually moved in with him into a bedsit and to do that we had to be Mr and Mrs, because even in the war these things were very frowned upon, I mean particularly as I was married to a serviceman. You've got to remember that we were living a very, very unnatural life. It wasn't an easy relationship for me. I had only recently lost my babe and I didn't realize I might be damaged, but the physical side of the relationship was always very painful. I was so enamoured of him, adored him, I never used to complain. And it was an important relationship at the time, it gave me some reason to get up in the morning hopefully. You weren't under a load of rubble, you had to be able to get through your intensely tiring day at work.

This went on, oh, for about fifteen months until I got sick. I had a complete physical breakdown. I collapsed at work and I was put off war work for the rest of the war.

It was then that Hughie showed how little he really cared. I was hospitalized for two weeks and he didn't come at all until the last day. He said he'd taken a room for me but that he wouldn't be able to be with me, he'd just come and visit. It was really, really shattering. I remember he took me and he showed me this room, four floors up in a really grotty place. I never saw him again.

It was at that stage that I started to think, it wasn't guilt exactly, it was shame, at what I'd done to my husband. I thought I was paying the price. I hadn't written to my husband all the time that I was living with Hughie, I'm not dishonest, I wouldn't have lied to him. But when Hughie left I wrote to him, a 'Dear John', which is really not very nice, tried to explain.

He was in Egypt at the time and he was so upset that he went to his commanding officer and told him all about it. This officer wrote to me. Well, I've never been torn off quite such a big strip, the whole letter was done on military papers. 'You should be totally and thoroughly ashamed of yourself to

The Second World War had opened up new horizons for women and even married women took advantage of this new freedom. About two-thirds of immediate post-war divorces were initiated by husbands, often based on the infidelity of their wives.

write such a letter to a serving man fighting for his country…' I began to feel about one inch high, very ashamed.

By the time my husband finally came back I felt nothing at all for him, he was like someone in a book. I went to meet him, he came off the boat and stood with his arms at his side. I felt nothing, absolutely nothing. We had this month's leave together and he tried every possible way to get me pregnant but it just didn't work. And in the end I knew I just couldn't live with him, all I would do is hurt him. So I left and I went to the Channel Islands where I stayed. He wouldn't divorce me for three years."

ALISON ASHFORD

Alison was born in 1926 in East London Transkei, South Africa, where her father was a medical missionary. She had two brothers and one sister. At the age of ten Alison was sent to school in England where she remained and later trained as a nurse. In 1948 she was working at Osborne House on the Isle of Wight when she met her future husband, Bill, who was recovering from his war wounds. The couple married the same year and then again in 1949. They had two daughters. The marriage ended in 1957 and Alison remarried a year later. She is now widowed and lives in Canterbury.

"I always had a romantic idea of love, my mother had brought me up on romantic novels like the ones by E. M. Dell and they gave such a perfect picture of love and marriage. So I really was a pushover for somebody with a little experience with women.

I met Bill when he was a patient in the hospital where I was working. Each patient had to come to my office for their medicine and somehow or other he used to come and have a special little word with me and after about three days he asked me if I would go out with him. And this was just the start of it all.

He had been serving in India and from what he told me had suffered a great deal. He told me that he had been married and that his wife had committed suicide and I was so very, very sorry for him. After I'd been out with him comparatively few times really he asked me if I would marry him. I just hadn't thought of marriage but suddenly I realized that I was in love with him and he kept telling me that he needed me so I agreed.

He asked if he could hurry the wedding along and set about getting a special licence. He hadn't tried to seduce me so I respected him for that tremendously. I didn't suspect there was any plan behind it. So I wrote to my mother and she telephoned me within a few hours of receiving my letter and she was utterly horrified. She said she had always planned her daughter's wedding and she wanted it to be a special affair. But Bill carried on organizing everything and in about ten days the wedding was arranged.

My mother came down the day before the wedding and I was very very nervous but he was charming to her. We sat up half the night my mother and I talking and she told me that she sensed there was something wrong and said, 'Please Alison, even now put it off even for a few weeks till I can know a little bit more about him.' I said that he really needed me. I was so in love that I believed everything he told me. I suppose he was very clever looking back on it.

It was a happy lovely service and our honeymoon was spent at Faringford House on the Isle of Wight. After this we went to London to live. It was all quite fun, quite crazy. We got a little bedsitter and we bought our cutlery at Woolworth's. We settled down into a routine.

He didn't need to work at that time because he was still on disability payment but after about three months we realized that something had to be done because we didn't have any money at all. Cheques started bouncing and we really got into debt. And it was then I guessed. I suppose I knew on the honeymoon but I'd pushed it to the back of my mind. He was a drinker, he could drink almost night and day without seeming the worse for it. He did get a little job in a garage and I had to go back to nursing.

I think we'd been married about five months when the really shattering part happened. There was a knock on the door and there was a man there in a fawn raincoat like you hear in the stories and he handed me a long brown envelope. I opened it and it was a petition for divorce from Bill's wife. I can't even really now explain what a shock it was. I knew he'd been married, I knew that his wife had committed suicide or I thought she had and yet he had never told me many details. There were pages of this thing. It said his wife was alive and living in India and she wanted a divorce because she knew all about the wedding to me. I realized that Bill had actually committed bigamy. I was horrified because to me it was the cardinal sin.

When Bill came in later I think I was in tears and I just handed him this petition. He said, 'Well, I wanted you and this was the only way.' But of course this was bigamy and therefore it was a matter for the police.

We went to Scotland Yard, we were interviewed. I think their main question was to me, 'Do you want to remain married?' Apart from the fact that I loved Bill very much I'd also discovered that I was pregnant so I said, 'Yes, of course I do.' Perhaps I thought that it was a bit romantic he wanted me so much that he risked all this.

**A nurse and a soldier pictured during the Second World War.
Alison Ashford met her husband in 1948 while she was working as a nurse at a hospital in the Isle of Wight.**

Above: Alison Ashford with her husband Bill in 1954. After six months of
marriage Alison discovered he was a bigamist.
Right: This photograph appeared in *Picture Post* magazine in 1951 as part of a
feature entitled Sex and the Citizen. The importance of sex in relationships was
beginning to be widely discussed at the time.

But I did keep it quiet and I can't remember telling anyone except my
family of course knew. And my brother who I adored didn't speak to me for
many, many years, it was just the shame of it.

Then Bill started staying out all night, sometimes coming back at about five
in the morning and I was worried stiff. I knew that he was drinking but I knew
there was something else, other women. My suspicions grew and he was beginning

to get careless. He would come back with lipstick on his collar and I could smell perfume. I didn't want to seem like the suspicious wife but on about the third night when he hadn't come home at all we did have a terrific row and I said I was sure that he was seeing other women. First of all he denied it, said I was imagining it and I was going to be like all possessive wives and then he admitted it.

At first I just felt sick. I didn't want to go to bed with him. Despite all that we'd got through Bill was still going out with other women and they were quite often prostitutes and this to me made it seem worse in a way. I tried to explain this to Bill and he listened and he was very sweet to me. Each time he said it was not going to happen again, he explained it was just a physical need and each time I believed him.

After nearly seven years I realized I'd had enough. Suddenly it had died. All the time until those last years I thought it was an illness and I should be able to help him more and I'd failed so hopelessly. I still believed that marriage should be forever but I knew it couldn't be."

BARBARA BAKER

Barbara was born in 1942 in Nantwich, Cheshire, and the family moved to Stoke-on-Trent when she was only a few years old. Her father worked as a chauffeur-gardener and she had two sisters and two brothers. In 1960 Barbara became pregnant and her parents sent her to work in a hospital as a cleaner and then on to have the baby in a Mother and Baby Home in Shrewsbury. Barbara was forced to have her son adopted when he was only six weeks old. Barbara had two more sons in 1963 and 1972. She was married for four years until 1967. However, she supported her sons alone by modelling and working as wardrobe mistress at the Victoria Theatre. In 1984 Barbara did a degree at her local college in Art and Design History and went on to do some lecturing there. She is now an alternative spiritual healer in Stoke-on-Trent.

"When we left school we were expected to get married and have children and live happily ever after, but that really wasn't something that I ever wanted. I wanted to go to art school but that was out of the question so really my life revolved around going to jazz clubs, dancing. The excitement of it all.

**Barbara Baker pictured in the late 1950s. During her affair
with a jazz musician she became pregnant and was forced to give
the baby up for adoption.**

When I was sixteen I went to London with my friend, we went for a
holiday, to do all the jazz clubs and coffee bars. It was kind of night and day, all
night sessions, jam sessions, exciting things and, whilst there, I met this
musician in one of the clubs. He was a very charismatic personality, he was also
something of an anarchist, not just in terms of being a musician, I mean he
himself. He was making his living out of his creativity and I think that was
probably the major thing which made him attractive to me. Somehow by being
with him I was half doing it myself.

Despite the new freedoms
of the 1950s, the old stigmas
surrounding extra-marital
affairs and illegitimacy
still remained.

I knew that he was married because obviously I sort of made my enquiries and people said, 'Oh no, you mustn't do that, he's a married man.' At first I felt maybe I was doing something wrong, but I sort of discarded all that. The whole thing was a rejection of all those values, Christian values. I thought I'd fallen in love you know and it didn't matter.

I knew that if my parents found out I'd be in terrible trouble but I didn't feel guilty about it. It wasn't really an issue with me. I didn't see marriage as a precious institution. I wasn't looking for a husband or a life partner or anything like that. It was just more, I suppose, living for now.

I kept it secret. Just one friend knew about it. I didn't talk to anybody about it, but I used to live for it really, I lived to meet him. I lived for the excitement of going to all these places where he would be playing up and down the country. The band used to tease me and call me the Renegade from Stoke, so you know they did acknowledge me as his girlfriend. All those sort of people, they themselves were rejecting the social norms, all these marriages were being questioned.

It was when I was eighteen that I actually became pregnant. I hadn't really had time to realize it before my mother guessed and so she sort of took over. My initial feelings were absolute terror really, and disbelief. I was just absolutely terrified of what people would do to me. It was decided by my parents to send me away from home. I was told not to tell anybody, I wasn't to tell my friends, not the people I worked with, nobody. I didn't tell the man himself. My mother said, 'Don't tell him because you don't want to ruin anybody else's life.' It was my problem, I must deal with it. Had he not been a married man they would have insisted on marrying me off, but because he was married that made them even more angry because that meant I was even more disgusting, even more immoral. I was selfish, didn't care about other people, I was willing to ruin somebody else's life, somebody's marriage.

And there was no question of me keeping this child, I must be sent away where nobody knows me and they sent me to a hospital where I worked as a cleaning woman from when I was five months to seven months pregnant. Then I was sent to a Mother and Baby Home which was run by the Church of England, and there we were very much made to do penance.

We had to work long hours and do chores, unnecessary chores, and we were treated like wicked women basically who had absolutely no say in our own destinies. We were not allowed any contact with the father of the child. And I was always seen as worse because this was a married man and I had defiled the sanctity of marriage. Not only had I already had sex when I wasn't married but I had, if you like, stepped on other people's territory. I had no morals and best locked away, kept away from society.

There was so much lack of human understanding, just sticking to the rules, no matter what. No allowance for human feelings whatsoever. We were just nobody in all this. There's no way we could be allowed to bring these children up. We were not given any counselling, we were simply told that you could stay at this home till the baby was six weeks old then you had to leave. Really you had no choice, you had to sign this document which said you give up all your rights as a mother to this child and that you will never try to contact them ever again, and they will be found good Christian families to go to.

I never agreed to it even though I signed those papers. I never verbally agreed to anything, I felt my life had been ruined. I felt that the only thing I ever would have to be mine was going to be taken away from me and I was meant to feel grateful, well I didn't. I felt that I was being robbed of something which was mine. I felt that half of me, more than half of me had been taken away. I felt like a dead person. My child had been stolen from me, that's how I saw it. I couldn't think about anything else, I couldn't feel anything else.

When I came home my father confronted me. I had a whole tirade of verbal abuse and the kind of language I'd never heard him speak before, he called me a threat to society. I was incredibly upset, of course, for my father of all people to call me all sorts of filth and that I should be locked up, and if the authorities wouldn't lock me away he would do it, he would lock me in the bedroom for two years and I wouldn't be able to go out, so I just left the next day. I felt the worst I've ever felt in my life. But I still didn't feel guilty about what I'd done and I think that made it worse, because I should have come home all sort of, you know, holding my head down and I didn't do that."

3

BLOODSHED AND BURNING

RIOTS

On 1 August 1919 four days and nights of looting and rioting began in Liverpool. There were no police on duty – they had come out on strike demanding recognition of their union. Poor families in the Scotland Road and dockland areas made the most of it, ransacking shops and helping themselves to meat, groceries, drink, clothing, boots and jewellery. Looters even raided music shops dragging pianos out into the streets, where – according to *The Times* – they 'thumped them in a frenzied endeavour to demonstrate their defiance of law and order'. A magistrate read the Riot Act from the turret of an armoured car. Tanks clattered through the shattered city shopping centre and troops fired volleys and advanced with bayonets to regain control of the city streets. In the end 370 arrests were made and many rioters were imprisoned with hard labour.

This disturbance was one in a series of riots which shook Britain in 1919. The riots began in January when some of the six million British soldiers awaiting demobilization staged strikes and violent demonstrations in army camps all over Britain. They were protesting about bad conditions in the camps and the delays in getting them back to 'Civvy Street' following the end of the First World War the previous year. They were also fearful that they were

---

An anti-German riot in High Street, Poplar, in London's East End, in May 1915. During a week of rioting over two thousand German properties were attacked.

about to be sent to Russia and deployed against the Red Army to defeat the revolution. Some of the most violent disturbances – for example those at Epsom and Chester in which several people were killed – involved Canadian troops who were waiting for arrangements to be made for their return home.

When the British soldiers were eventually demobilized, however, there was often further trouble. There was no sign of the homes for heroes they had been promised, often not even a job to return to. Bitterly disappointed groups of demobbed soldiers rioted in Wolverhampton, Salisbury, Swindon and elsewhere during the spring and early summer of 1919. One of the most serious incidents involving British ex-servicemen occurred in Luton where the town hall was set on fire and shops were looted. The police station was besieged and the crowd was only cleared by a baton charge with 100 civilian casualities.

Then in May and June 1919 there were race riots in a number of British seaports where several thousand black people had settled during the war. Here again unemployment after the war was an important triggering factor. The black newcomers had worked as seamen and dockers but now the war was over they were seen as a threat to the jobs and the wages of the white workers. There was also much sexual envy at the success black sailors were having with local white women. Riots occurred in London, Liverpool, Tyneside, Hull, Glasgow, Cardiff, Newport and Barry. The black sailors' lodging houses were besieged, stormed, and emptied of furniture which was then burnt in street bonfires. In Limehouse, East London and in Liverpool, guns, knives and razors were used in the battles. But the most serious disturbances occurred in Cardiff in June. Three people were killed, dozens were hospitalized and £3000 worth of damage was inflicted on property in the city. The police offered little protection to the black community under siege – but the overwhelming reaction of the press was to blame them for what was happening. In the aftermath of the riots the government introduced a repatriation scheme to remove the 'threat' to public order posed by the presence of the black sailors. They were offered a resettlement allowance of £5 with a further voyage allowance of £1. In the months that followed about 1500 men sailed off to the Caribbean and West Africa under this scheme.

The history of race relations in Britain in the twentieth century is not one of tolerance, generosity and liberal attitudes. During the early years of the century small-scale race riots were quite common. Russian Jewish communities which had developed in major cities like Manchester, Leeds and in East London were targets for violent hostility. Even tiny Jewish communities like

Troops are brought into Liverpool during the transport workers' strike of 1911. This year saw the highpoint of industrial violence in Britain.

that in South Wales could be attacked. In August 1911 violence broke out in Tredegar and in the next week spread to Ebbw Vale, Rhymney, Bargoed, and elsewhere, resulting in £16 000 worth of damage (over a million pounds worth of damage by today's values). The main underlying grievance which triggered these riots was competition for jobs and homes, and resentment against the prosperity of Jewish shopkeepers and tradesmen.

During the First World War the German community in Britain was the target of widespread racial violence. Wartime propaganda helped to create an image of all Germans as evil and warmongering – even those who had lived in England for generations. Anti-German disturbances broke out on five occasions, between August 1914 and July 1917. The worst riots occurred in May 1915, sparked off by the sinking of the passenger liner *Lusitania* by a German submarine with the loss of over 1000 lives. German shopkeepers were targeted and attacked in almost every town and city in Britain. In a week of rioting in London over 2000 German properties were attacked, £200 000 worth of damage was done (by today's values, around £20 million), 900 people were arrested and there were hundreds injured. Between 1914 and 1918 the 50 000 strong German community had to endure what was probably one of the most sustained attacks on any immigrant community in recent British history.

Hostility towards another, far more numerous ethnic minority, the Irish, was another source of civil disturbances and riots in the early decades of the century. The hostility was most intense during the Victorian era when Irish immigration was at its height, but the violence continued into the inter-war years especially in Liverpool and Glasgow, both of which had large Irish populations. The fundamental cause was religion and, in particular, a deep-rooted anti-Catholicism. The riots were essentially sectarian battles between the militant Orange Order of Protestants against Catholics of Irish descent. Most were triggered by the ritual Orange Day marches on 12 July or by Catholic marches on St Patrick's Day. Each side had their own drum bands, their own battle hymns and their own uniforms and ceremonial costumes all of which added emotion to these events. With anything up to 50 000, dressed up in full regalia the marches provided an awesome spectacle and could take up to an hour to pass a given point. Marching was a primal way of asserting physical strength and making territorial claims on a neighbourhood. Every year this would be contested and ridiculed by the other side. In Edwardian Liverpool this religious pageantry sparked off regular riots, the worst of which occurred in 1909 when there were several weeks of serious Protestant-Catholic violence. More minor disturbances recurred in the 1920s and 1930s. In inter-war Glasgow not a July passed without a significant outbreak of violence, involving many injuries and arrests. Every year the headlines in the *Sunday Mail* following the Orange Day parades had a familiar ring: 'Glasgow Orange Day Riot: 50 arrests' (1925); 'Many arrests follow Orange Walk' (1927); 'Scottish Orange Day Tragedies' (1930). These troubles were additionally fuelled by the traditional sectarian rivalry between Glasgow's two main football teams, Celtic (closely linked with the Catholic community) and Rangers (closely linked with the established church in Scotland and the Orange Lodges). Fixtures between Rangers and Celtic provided ritual opportunities for tribal war between the rival supporters before, during or after the matches. The battles between bottle-throwing contingents of supporters, many of them driven by religious hatred, formed a constant threat to public order in Glasgow on big match days. Occasionally – as in the Scottish Cup Final between Celtic and Rangers in 1909 – fan violence could lead to a major riot.

Crowd disorder at football matches was quite common in the early part of the century. Crowd control and policing at matches was very basic, making pitch invasions very easy for fans. Some invaded to celebrate, others to disrupt the match. In 1906 the Spurs-Aston Villa cup tie had to be abandoned after spectators 'swarmed onto the turf at the interval… and a violent crowd formed in front of the stand'. The most well-known case of football crowd disorder is the 1923 Cup Final when around 250 000 people invaded the new 127 000 capacity Wembley stadium and spilled onto the pitch. Although the pitch was cleared by a now legendary lone policeman on a white horse, it is often forgotten that after the match the Royal Box was invaded and ransacked by fans in search of souvenirs. The type of crowd disorder most frequently reported at this time, however, was attacks on players and match officials. Between 1921 and 1939 seventy-two cases of spectator disorder were reported to the Football Association, leading to the temporary closure of eight grounds. Little fuss was made by the police or the press about these outbreaks of violence at football matches – they were seen as part of the game.

Much more concern was expressed about civil disturbances that surrounded violent strikes. In the 1900s strikes were often violent affairs in which there was much damage inflicted on property and many were injured. Baton-wielding police would try to protect 'blackleg labour' brought in by employers from the attacks of strikers and pickets. There were normally close links between the owners of industry, the chief constables and the local magistrates all of which added to the sense that a class war was being fought on the streets. During the Tonypandy riot of November 1910 the battle between striking South Wales miners and the police continued for several days leaving 200 casualties. During the riots all the shops in the village were looted. Occasionally, the army was called in by the government to restore order, often with disastrous consequences. Soldiers were despatched, for example, to South Wales during the national railway strike of July 1911, provoking furious rioting in Llanelli. Troops of the Worcester Regiment opened fire on a stone-throwing

Members of the Civil
Constabulary Reserve Force
which was formed during the
General Strike of 1926.
Although the strike was
represented in newsreels and
newspapers as being peaceful,
there were some violent clashes
between police and strikers.

crowd, killing three after a train had been boarded by strikers trying to force the driver and fireman from the footplate. In August, Home Secretary Winston Churchill called out 50000 armed troops to deal with disorder in London and Liverpool as the transport workers' strike spread.

1911 was the highpoint of industrial violence in Britain. After this the government tended to adopt a more conciliatory approach to industrial relations and encouraged more even-handed police methods. Strikes were never as violent again. In moments of conflict, though, the old enmity between strikers and police sometimes resurfaced. The General Strike of 1926, for example, was represented in the newsreels and newspapers of the time as a week of good-humoured sporting fixtures between police and strikers. In fact the week produced 3149 prosecutions for incitement to sedition and for violence in England and Wales. In some cases the police over-reacted in the most petty way. In Accrington a small boy was prosecuted for throwing orange peel at a charabanc. Actions like this and the arrest of a woman from Heath in Nottinghamshire for chalking 'don't be a scab' on the road sometimes triggered violent reprisals. In some of the most militant mining villages – known in the press as 'Little Moscows' because of the communist leanings of the inhabitants – there were frequent clashes with the police during the strike. One such 'Little Moscow' was the village of Mardy in South Wales where the local women – conspicuous on the picket lines – posed the main problem for the special police drafted into the Rhondda to keep order. But the defeat of the General Strike marked a watershed in industrial relations. After 1926, trade unions, with much reduced membership levels, became more cautious and conservative. Strikes, and especially violent strikes, became far less common.

From the late 1920s onwards unemployment was on the increase and conflict between the unemployed and the police provided the next major wave of riots on the city streets. The most violent period of conflict between the unemployed and the police was in the early 1930s when unemployment peaked at around four million. It was triggered by government legislation in 1931 which reduced benefits to the unemployed and introduced the family means test. Almost half a million people immediately lost their right to benefit

---

The *Flying Scotsman* after it had been derailed by striking miners in 1926 near Cramlington in Northumberland. During the General Strike volunteers had been running the railways. Although nobody was seriously hurt in the derailment four miners were jailed for eight years.

Police charge Hunger March demonstrators in Hyde Park. The marchers who had come from all over the country were met by five thousand police, such was the official paranoia about the activities of the unemployed movement at that time.

altogether. Anger at these cuts swelled the ranks of the communist-led National Unemployed Workers Movement, formed by Walter Hannington in 1921. The NUWM grew to about 35 000 members in over 300 branches. Demonstrations were organized all over Britain to draw attention to the plight of the unemployed and to demand a better deal for those out of work. The government, fearful of a communist plot to undermine or overthrow it, responded with brute force: mounted police charges against the protesters were a common feature of these demonstrations. During the winter of 1931–2 there were violent clashes between the police and the unemployed in over thirty

towns and cities as far afield as Bristol, Castleford, Manchester and Glasgow. In the turmoil which followed there was often looting of shops and warehouses, confirming the worst fears of the authorities. One of the most violent riots occurred in Birkenhead in September 1932. It began when the police attacked a demonstration of around 10 000 people who had marched to Birkenhead Public Assistance Committee to demand an increase in the rate of unemployment relief. The battle between the demonstrators and the police continued for the next three days and nights with widespread looting. The NUWM leaders quickly lost control over the conflict and in the violence that followed many old scores were settled – between Protestants and Catholics, between Catholics and the police, and between white and ethnic workers on the docks. In the aftermath of the Birkenhead riots two local NUWM leaders received prison sentences of two years.

It was in this atmosphere of official paranoia about the threat to public order posed by the unemployed that the early hunger marches to London took place. On 19 October 1932, as the Home Secretary denounced the subversive activities of the NUWM, eighteen contingents of its members marched on London as part of the 'Great National Hunger March against the Means Test' which was to present a petition of a million signatures to Parliament. Police spies and Special Branch infiltrators who had penetrated the NUWM reported back on the dangers of its call for 'mass struggle on the streets'. When the marchers and their sympathizers arrived in Hyde Park on 27 October they were met by 5000 police. A battle ensued which spread onto the surrounding streets and seventy-five people were reported injured. There were further disturbances in the next week which led to more injuries, more damage to property and around fifty arrests. The hunger marches to London continued through the 1930s accompanied by skirmishes with the police when they arrived in Hyde Park. But by the mid-1930s unemployment was falling and the NUWM had lost much of its drive and its membership.

A new focus for public disorder in the mid-1930s was Sir Oswald Mosley's British Union of Fascists. To begin with the BUF, formed in 1932, was eminently respectable and was supported by the *Daily Mail* in its campaign 'Hurrah for the Blackshirts'. But by 1934 Mosley was beginning to emulate Hitler's violence towards the Jews, whipping up anti-Semitic feeling in hundreds of street-corner political meetings, especially in London's East End. Although Mosley only attracted limited support, the Jewish community felt extremely vulnerable to verbal and physical attacks by the BUF who marched the streets – often armed – in their blackshirt uniforms, chanting anti-Semitic slogans. The Communist Party presented the most immediate and vociferous opposition to this bullying and many young Jews joined, prepared to fight back. After many skirmishes the conflict between fascists and Jewish anti-fascists came to a head on 4 October 1936 in what became known as the 'Battle of Cable Street'. When the fascists organized a march through a Jewish quarter of the East End, the Labour Party advised opponents to stay at home. The Communist Party, however, adopted a policy of direct opposition on the streets and organized a counter-demonstration of about 100 000 supporters, many of

**Fascists saluting Sir Oswald Mosley in Bermondsey in 1938.
The members of the British Union of Fascists staged violent attacks on the
Jewish community in London.**

them Jewish. Barricades were thrown across the streets by the Communist
opposition and many fights broke out, including a major flare-up in Cable
Street, Shadwell, before the march was finally abandoned. Much less widely
reported were the smaller-scale battles between fascists and communists
regularly fought out on Saturday nights in cities like Newcastle, Leeds and
Manchester in the thirties.

Government concern over the threat posed by anti-fascist riots and
continuing protests by the unemployed led to the passing of the Public Order
Act which became operative in 1937. The wearing of political uniform was

A skirmish with police during a fascist march to Trafalgar Square in 1937.

banned. The police were given far greater control over marches and demonstrations – including the right to ban them – and it became illegal to carry offensive weapons at public meetings.

The main disturbances during and after the Second World War continued to be associated with race. In June 1940 there were violent attacks on the Italian communities in London, Liverpool, South Wales and Scotland following the entry of Mussolini's Italy into the war against Britain. These riots however were far less severe than the anti-German disturbances during the First World War. In August 1947 there were anti-Semitic riots in Liverpool, Manchester and Glasgow with widespread looting of Jewish shops and factories. The next year there were riots directed against the 8000-strong black community which had grown up in Liverpool during the war. Then, after a decade of black immigration into Britain to fill the labour shortage at home, there were renewed race riots in August and September 1958 in Nottingham and London's Notting Hill. Behind many of these disturbances lay white working-class fears about unemployment and the scapegoating of immigrant groups as the cause of the problem. They were often triggered by the failure of the police to protect the new settlers from this hostility. But, as in 1919, it was the black newcomers who were blamed. In the wake of the riots came a successful Conservative Party campaign for the introduction of tight controls on immigration.

FREDA PHILP

Freda's family moved to Epsom when she was four years old in 1908 when her father became the Inspector of Epsom Police Force. Freda and her six sisters and two brothers lived with their parents above the police station. In 1919 Freda had just started work at the local greengrocer's. A year later she left to work at the Co-op where she remained until she was sixty. After her retirement Freda married. She is now widowed and still lives in Epsom.

"The war was over, you see, and the soldiers were more or less just killing time there. They used to come down from the camp at Woodcote Park and spent their money in the town, in the pubs. Usually ended in a fight in the pub, you see. It was the mood they were in I suppose, frustrated that they were being kept waiting so long before they could go home.

On this particular night two of the soldiers were causing a lot of disturbance in one of the pubs, quarrelling, fighting. The publican called the police and the two men were arrested, taken to the station and put in the cells. Word got back to the camp and all the others got together and came down to try to free their friends.

They all came down in hordes, about four or five hundred of them. On the way they pulled down fences, gathered up stones and bricks and, of course, they threw these through our windows. They trampled all over our front garden, pulled the railings down. They ripped the iron bars out of the windows and they tried to get into the cells.

Freda Philp photographed
in 1916.

Epsom police station where
Freda's father was the inspector
and where her family lived. The
photograph was taken the day
after the riot by Canadian
soldiers in June 1919.

**A damaged cell door inside the police station where the soldiers had
attempted to break in during the riot.**

There were only a very few men on duty. My father was on duty and my
brother was home on leave, waiting for his demob from the army, so he went
down to help stop them getting in.

I was upstairs with my little brother, three sisters and my mother, and
course I was in bed. There was no way of getting out, you see, 'cos our only way
of exit was through the front door of the station. So Mum pushed us little ones
into a little cupboard between the bedrooms. It was the only safe place where
we could get away from the glass and the stones.

It seemed endless to us, I know I was terrified myself. I was very
frightened, shed a few tears because, as I say, they were throwing stones and
bricks through the windows and we had no protection you see. The noise was
terrific. They were all shouting and well, what with breaking glass and shouting
and screaming, I was too frightened. It seemed an endless night.

They didn't actually get in the station. The military police eventually arrived and they were all rounded up and sent back to the camp.

But Dad had a big gash on the back of his head which had to have stitches, seven or eight stitches, quite a nasty gash. There were several of them who had head injuries you see. Sergeant Green was taken to hospital but very sadly he died the next morning of his injuries."

NELLIE WALLACE

Nellie was born in 1911 in Liverpool and had a sister and a brother. Her father was a seaman and her mother worked as a hospital cleaner. At the age of just ten Nellie started work as a barrow girl working with a handcart selling fruit and vegetables around the streets. She married when she was eighteen. Her husband was unemployed and Nellie brought up their eleven children single-handed. Nellie still lives in Liverpool.

"Every shop was smashed in, everyone breaking the windows and picking stuff up wasn't they, tins of corned beef, tins of everything. We had pieces of lovely bacon in the street and the people was hungry, I seen them all running, all the gear, carrying it on their shoulders. Oh, me mam got jewels out the pawnshop, shawls and people's bundles were gettin' thrown out the pawnshop. I seen men carrying new boots, shoes, then the next was a clothes shop, next door was a pickle shop. The meat shop, that got done, all the legs of lamb, bread shop, all the cakes, them cakes was nice though, boxes of 'em thrown through the window.

You'd see all the things all scattered around and everyone run with the stuff in their hands, running to plant it, hide it. When you got into Scotland Road all the stuff was thrown out through the windows and everything breaking. It was like, like a riot you know.

It was terrible though, 'twas really, and then, when the soldiers come oh we had to run and get in our houses quick. They'd show you the baton, the gun, well you run away when you see a gun don't you? What d'you call it? A curfew, we couldn't get out then.

They come down searching and banging yer doors in to see what stolen goods you had in the house and all the kids screaming. Not one soldier, about

LOOTING AT LIVERPOOL: TROOPS; TANKS; A WAR-SHIP IN THE MERSEY.

PHOTOGRAPHS BY TOPICAL AND ILLUSTRATIONS BUREAU

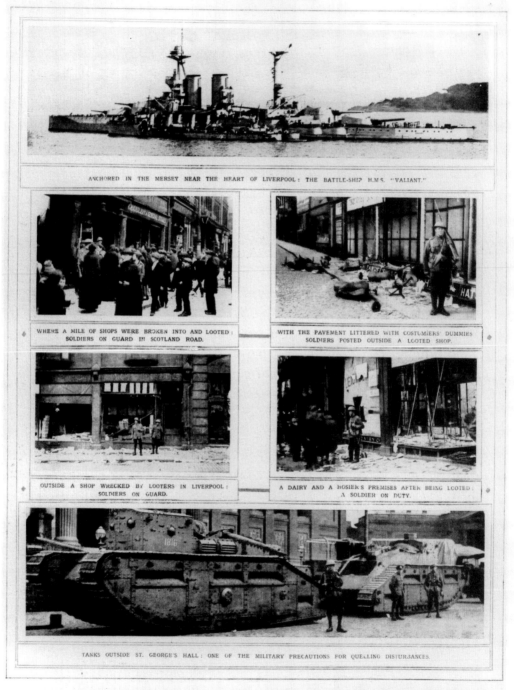

ANCHORED IN THE MERSEY NEAR THE HEART OF LIVERPOOL: THE BATTLE-SHIP H.M.S. "VALIANT."

WHERE A MILE OF SHOPS WERE BROKEN INTO AND LOOTED: SOLDIERS ON GUARD IN SCOTLAND ROAD.

WITH THE PAVEMENT LITTERED WITH COSTUMIERS' DUMMIES: SOLDIERS POSTED OUTSIDE A LOOTED SHOP.

OUTSIDE A SHOP WRECKED BY LOOTERS IN LIVERPOOL: SOLDIERS ON GUARD.

A DAIRY AND A HOSIER'S PREMISES AFTER BEING LOOTED: A SOLDIER ON DUTY.

TANKS OUTSIDE ST. GEORGE'S HALL: ONE OF THE MILITARY PRECAUTIONS FOR QUELLING DISTURBANCES.

Following on the recent strike of police in Liverpool, serious rioting broke out in that city on August 2, and the mob took advantage of the depletion of the forces of law and order to break through the windows of shops and loot their contents. In Scotland Road, it was reported, shop-fronts were thus wrecked for a distance of more than a mile, and similar scenes took place in London Road and other parts of that locality. The police who had remained on duty, assisted by "Specials," made baton charges. There were also bayonet charges by troops, and a volley was fired over the heads of the crowd. On the 5th it was stated that Liverpool was surrounded by a military cordon. Tanks were posted outside St. George's Hall, and the battle-ship "Valiant" anchored in the Mersey, in readiness for eventualities. Nearly 370 arrests were made.

five to six to the one house. They searched everything, even dragged yer beds out to see if there was any loot. My mum had this big long john full of bacon and she has it on the fire. And the soldier says, 'What are you boiling?' She says, 'Old towels.'

Well then the next day our neighbour, Annie, she said, 'Come on with me Nellie'. She took me to this grave and I thought she was puttin' flowers on the grave. Well she takes the vase out and takes out this chamois leather thing with all jewels in it and she said to the grave, 'Now mind that 'til I come back'. It was her husband's grave, that was a good plant wasn't it?"

ERNEST MARKE

Ernest grew up in Sierra Leone where he was born in 1902. At the age of fifteen he stowed away on a ship bound for England and never saw his family again. In 1919, after two years with the British navy he settled in Liverpool working on the docks. Due to the violence of the race riots Ernest accepted the British government's offer of 'repatriation'. He was sent on a passage to British Guyana and for a short time worked in the sugar-cane fields there. Later Ernest travelled throughout the world working in various jobs from ship's stoker to magician. He married twice and has six children. Ernest now lives in London.

"I was just demobilized from the army so I was in civvies and I went around the corner to buy a Snapper as it was my turn to cook. Suddenly a crowd says, 'Here's one of them niggers, get him.' Oh my God, I started running and good job I wasn't far off where my house was but before I could get there some women with clogs on and shawls over their heads pulled out and says to this mob, 'Leave him alone, he hasn't done anything to you'. So I got away.

On another occasion myself and this boy from St Lucia we got off the bus at Lime Street, walking towards the Adelphi Hotel, when suddenly this crowd saw us, like a pack of wolves they started chasing us. They was shouting, 'Black

A page from the *Illustrated London News* depicting the aftermath of the riots during the Liverpool police strike in August 1919.

bastard, nigger.' We really were frightened. Again it was a woman who saved me. She heard the noise and opened her window telling us to go round the corner and through the back alley, she opened the back gate for us and in we went. The crowd passed, they couldn't find us. I really thought we were gonna be killed that time and I had actually knew this bloke who was killed with the riot you see, killed by one of these crowds.

After that I bought a razor, most of the boys carried razors, not to hurt anyone but just for their own protection. And when the next mob started coming towards me they cornered me so I pulled out this razor and started slashing, they ran. The moment they left me I ran like mad put the razor back and saw the blood, found I'd cut meself so I said, 'No more razor for me.' Threw it away. After, I carried a gun for a hell of a long time for my protection.

The police can't help you, some of them was as bad, very prejudiced. They gotta kick the lower person and who was the lower person, the negro.

We'd meet in the evening, 'What happened to you?' and everybody would tell their experiences of how they got beat up or whatever. The fear was in our eyes, there's no subject except the riot.

It wasn't really hatred of the blacks you see, it's jobs, we were just a scapegoat. They just come from the army and they forget we also come from the front line, well, that's the human race see, they're selfish. And most of the white men, they're jealous of their women, thinking that their wife or their daughters will… so they hate us immediately. Sexual jealousy is there, 'I don't want my daughter going with a goddamn nigger.' The hatred just comes automatically. One or two just want violence but they're the biggest cowards of all, they'll run like mad if they're not a mob.

The government began to realize that they must get rid of us or there was going to be a lot of bloodshed. So any black man they see they give him a pamphlet and tell him to go to a meeting, a lecture in the big building there in Fleet Street. I went and I heard this white man from the Colonial Office giving this lecture to us, 'You think the country's getting too hot for you so we can give you a free passage home, and we'll give each one of you one pound now to get your things out of the pawnshop and five more when you land ashore.' They used the word 'repatriation' and then they started preaching to us about the countries we could go to and gold in abundance, British Guyana, diamonds in various sizes. So I said, 'You'd better send me there.'

I wanted to see the world and I was glad to leave those troubles in Liverpool. But when I got off the ship in Guyana it was like jumping out of the frying-pan into the fire. The only job I could get was in the sugar-cane fields. I think it was four cents a bed, terrible. I asked a man, I said, 'Where's the diamonds? Where's the gold?' But he said that was up-country where there were lots of snakes big enough to swallow a goat. Well, I said, 'I'd rather stay here than go meet all those big snakes 'cos I'm smaller than a goat.' So I never went.

It was all deception, the government realized that the country was getting out of control and they thought well the best way to do is to get them home, forcing us out."

STANLEY JONES

Stanley was born in 1917 in Birkenhead where his father worked as a docker. At the time of the unemployment riot in 1932 Stanley had left school and was working on a milk round. At the age of sixteen he got a job at Camel Laird's shipbuilders where he remained for the rest of his working life. Stanley has been married twice and has four children. He still lives in Birkenhead with his second wife.

"Me dad was a staunch Orangeman so he got me to join the Orange Lads. We were taught in the Orange Lodge to hate all Catholics and when we used to get the day off from school on the twelfth of July we used to get dressed in our orange outfit, line up outside the Orange Hall and be in a big long procession with all banners.

The Catholics were there and they were jeering and mocking, I used to stick me tongue out at them, I even used to spit on 'em. Used to be hundreds there waitin' for us and they'd start fightin', throwing bottles, glass, bricks, and even tiles off the roof would come hurtling down and we'd run 'cos the Catholics they outnumbered us.

On one twelfth of July they picked me out to be Orangeman, King Billy, to ride this horse in the procession. It started off, me on this horse at the front and somebody threw a stone and it hit me right on the 'ead and I fell off the 'orse. I looked a right banana, all sprawled over there, and the horse belted off. I've got this big hat on and a sword, a dummy sword like. I could hear the band and everybody was laughing you know, 'cos all me clothes was dirty, 'cos I'd fell into horse muck, so I started wading into the crowd, into the Catholics. There was a right turmoil, all the band they were playing the flutes and they started hitting out with the flutes. And I started hitting out with this sword. There was blood everywhere, I'd actually blooded people.

But then we always got our revenge on them on St Patrick's day. We'd get up a group and go up to their school, when they come out to play we used to lambast them. Me boots, they were studded at the bottom to save the leather, the toes was steel-capped. And we used to just literally charge through them, used to kick them, even the girls I used to kick saying, 'I'm kicking you because I can't see yer brother.' They used to be bleeding down their legs. The teachers used to come down to the Protestant school and complain about it. Well, they did the same thing to us so really it was just a matter of tit for tat.

I was brought up to believe it. You see me grandfather used to tell me about the Catholics, not to have anything to do with them, but I used to have a lot of Catholic mates living in the back. I used to play with them, to me they were all right, but me dad, if ever he caught me, he used to belt me."

CHARLIE GOODMAN

Charlie was born in 1915 in Camden, North London. His father was killed in the First World War and Charlie was cared for by various uncles and aunts until he moved to Stepney in the East End to become an apprentice silversmith when he was fourteen.

After the Battle of Cable Street in 1936 Charlie joined the International Brigade and fought in Spain from January 1937 until February 1938. On his return to Britain he joined the Communist Party and during the Second World War served in the air force.

Charlie and his wife Joy married in 1941 and have two sons and a daughter. After the war he worked on the London Underground. Charlie has for many years been an elected representative of the local tenants' housing association and still gives talks in community colleges and schools on the problems of racism.

"There was a generation, the old people, that believed in the police. You should keep your head down, we shouldn't go to stop Mosley. In fact, the *Jewish Chronicle* had a centre page which said, 'Stay at home, close your windows. Don't take part, keep a low profile.' This was ignored and we all went.

There were thousands there at Gardners' Corner but we didn't see a fascist the whole day long, we only saw the police. The fascists were drawn up in Royal Mint Street being reviewed by Mosley and they never got any further.

The streets were very, very narrow at that time and they had a lot of warehouses and lock-up places, which we forced open and pulled out lorries, carts and things. We overturned them and made barricades ready to block Mosley's way through.

Then the police charged the barricades but above were tenements and the women just leaned out from there, threw everything they could lay their hands on down on to the police, and when I say everything I mean everything: hot water, boiling water, kitchen oil, fat, urine, lumps of shit, anything they could lay their hands on. And the coppers got the full force of it so they ran to hide in some sheds. And then a lot of women came down and started banging on the shed doors and kicking at the shed doors, and with that groups of police came out with their hands up in the air and surrendering. Well, whoever saw a policeman surrender? What do you do? So we took their helmets and told them to shove off.

The rest of the police got very panicked and some of them were stood there going 'Heil Hitler' and that sort of thing, which was very provocative. Then somebody threw a brick through this coach and that was when the police started bashing, battening, right left and centre and they pushed the people back a little way. They was just indiscriminately battering people, knocking people through plate-glass windows or shops.

Because people were frightened they began to go back as far as they could so I climbed up the lamppost, and I said, 'Come on, these are our streets, let's defend them, don't be pushed back, come forward.' And the people came forward.

The mounted police was whacking away with laths, whacking away at my legs though they couldn't bring me down, and finally, when I did begin to come down I was just swept behind the crowd. The police was still battering away and one policeman was just about to whack a woman on the head so I punched him in the face. Anyway I was arrested and about twelve or fourteen police took me to the station. Well when they got me there they turned me up like a battering ram and they just bashed the charge room door open with my head, beating me with truncheons all shouting out, 'You yellow bastard.' When I came round again I had about twelve stitches in my head and in my pocket there was a brick, a file, a bag of shot which were planted on me while I was unconscious. And I was charged with incitement to riot, carrying dangerous weapons, assaulting the police. I was sent to prison for four months hard labour."

Charlie Goodman being arrested during the Battle of Cable Street on 4 October 1936. Charlie received a four-month prison sentence for his part in the demonstration to prevent the fascists from marching through London's East End.

BARON BAKER

Baron, born in 1925 in Port Antonia, Jamaica, had three brothers and a sister. Their father was a wharf official. Baron joined the Royal Air Force when he was fifteen by telling them that he was a year older. In 1944, after serving in the RAF for four years, he arrived in Britain and settled in London where he got a job working as a labourer on the railways. In 1958 at the time of the riots Baron was living in Notting Hill where he was involved in anti-fascist activities and in the campaign for better housing for the West Indian community. He is single and still lives in West London.

"Mosley tried to stir up a conflict between the blacks and the whites because his aim was to drive the blacks from North Kensington, to drive them from the shores of England. I wasn't for that because I came here to fight for the mother country...

Mosley was stirring up a hate campaign, his supporters, the Teddy boys running around with bicycle chains and 'Keep Britain White, Keep Britain White'. They were going around in groups seeking out a coloured and beating him up, fighting, repressing coloured man or coloured woman, they go round kicking them about and beating them up. Well, black people were so frightened at that time that they wouldn't leave their house, they wouldn't come out, they wouldn't walk the streets of Portobello Road.

So we decided to form a defence force to fight against that type of behaviour and we did. We organized a force to take home coloured people wherever they were living in the area. We were not leaving our homes and going out attacking anyone, but if you attack our homes you would be met, that was the type of defence force we had.

We were warned when they were coming and we had a posse to guard our headquarters. When they told us that they were coming to attack that night I went around and told all the people that was living in the area to withdraw

---

Police searching a man on the streets of Notting Hill in London in 1958. In August and September of that year there were violent race riots in London and Nottingham.

that night. The women I told them to keep pots, kettles of hot water boiling, get some caustic soda and anyone tried to break down the door and come in just lash out with them. The men, well we were armed. During the day they went out and get milk bottles, get what they could find and get the ingredients of making the Molotov cocktail bombs. Make no mistake, there were iron bars, there were machetes, there were all kinds of arms, weapons, we had guns.

We made preparations at the headquarters for the attack. We had men on the housetop waiting for them, I was standing on the second floor with the lights out as look-out when I saw a massive lot of people out there. I was observing the behaviour of the crowd outside from behind the curtains upstairs and they say, 'Let's burn the niggers, let's lynch the niggers.' That's the time I gave the order for the gates to open and throw them back where they were coming from. I was an ex-serviceman, I knew guerrilla warfare, I knew all about their game and it was very, very effective. I says, 'Start bombing them.' When they saw the Molotov cocktails coming and they start to panic and run. It was a very serious bit of fighting that night, we were determined to use any means, any weapon, anything at our disposal for our freedom. We were not prepared to go down like dying dogs.

But it did work, we gave Sir Oswald Mosley and his Teddy boys such a whipping they never come back in Notting Hill. I knew one thing, the following morning we walked the streets free because they knew we were not going to stand for that type of behaviour."

4

SLAVE CAMPS AND SKIVVY SCHOOLS

UNEMPLOYMENT

In the late 1930s, unemployed young people were invited by labour exchanges to free viewings of a Ministry of Labour propaganda film, *On the Way to Work*. It was one of the first official films to try to sell a government retraining scheme to unemployed youth. The images showed cloth-capped youngsters plucked from dole queues enjoying themselves by day chopping down trees and damming streams, then relaxing by night playing darts and singing in a scout-camp-type setting.

The reality was very different. Known to the inmates as 'slave camps' these government work camps were one of the most unpopular of all the inter-war schemes for the unemployed. The first opened in Presteigne in Mid Wales in 1929 and ten years later there were thirty-five of them designed (in the official jargon of the time) to 'recondition' around 25 000 young inmates each year. In all, around 150 000 young men on the dole – most of them aged between eighteen and twenty-five – passed through these harsh and punitive institutions in the 1930s. They were the centrepiece of an interlocking system of work camps and training centres which were designed to deal with the new problem of mass unemployment and to get the unemployed back to work. Unemployment between the wars was higher than ever before in Britain. In the worst years of the depression in the early 1930s there were almost four million out of work. The problem was made worse by much long-term structural unemployment in the old industries of the first Industrial Revolution

Queues at a labour exchange in 1935. The unemployed had to sign on twice a week to be eligible for the dole.

such as coal-mining, cotton, iron and steel, and shipbuilding which were concentrated in South Wales, the north of England and Scotland.

The aim of the work camps was to instil a basic physical and mental discipline in young people who were thought to have lost the will to work – complaints about scroungers and dole abuse were as widespread then as today. They were dispatched to the camps – Nissen hut colonies on Forestry Commission land – for a three-month stint of military-style discipline and pick-and-shovel labour. The working day normally began at six in the morning, and after ritually saluting the Union Jack the inmates would spend ten to twelve hours felling trees, ditching, hedging, planting or road-making, overseen by retired sergeant majors and police officers. The living conditions were spartan and in the evenings and weekends there was little to do as the camps were deliberately built in remote spots like Brechfa in Carmarthenshire or Glenbranter in Argyllshire, far from the temptations of the pub and the dance hall. For their trouble the inmates received two or three shillings and a packet of Woodbines per week.

Recruitment was voluntary to begin with and young men arrived by the lorry load with high hopes of a new future as the labour exchanges had promised them a good chance of a proper job when they completed the course. A few did move on to trainee schemes in the early 1930s, helping to build Whipsnade Zoo and the extension to the Piccadilly Line. But there was little co-operation from employers and schemes like this soon broke down.

When the three-month course was completed most returned to the dole queues in the mining villages and declining manufacturing towns where they had come from. The tendency of bosses to look down on youngsters who had gone to labour camps as hopeless cases further undermined the scheme. Horror stories about the 'slave camps' also quickly circulated amongst the unemployed adding to their unpopularity. For a time the scheme became compulsory and labour exchanges threatened to stop the benefit money of those who refused to go. Yet by the late 1930s almost one in every three young men sent to the labour camps quit or was discharged before completing the full course – despite the fact that they would not be able to claim when they returned home. The word amongst the young unemployed was that you were much more likely to get a job if you stayed at home and kept your contacts fresh rather than suffer the stigma of being a 'slave camper'.

Some of those in the dole queues saw emigration to the Commonwealth and Empire colonies as their best chance of getting a job. Emigration had traditionally offered the hope of a new life to the poor and the unemployed. During the first decades of the century around 200 000 sailed away each year to live permanently overseas, most of them heading for Britain's colonies which were hungry for white settlers to work as farm labourers and domestic servants. This mass exodus – apart from the deportation of convicts – was generally a voluntary and private matter. It was encouraged by more than fifty voluntary organizations (most of them religious) like the Salvation Army, YMCA and the Church Emigration Society, which helped with assisted passages and loans. Emigration was seen as a way of binding the dominions with blood ties, it was an instrument for spreading the Christian gospel and way of life to the most distant parts of the Empire, and it seemed to offer a solution to the problem of unemployment at home. As unemployment increased so emigration began to attract more and more official government interest and involvement.

Under the 1905 Unemployed Workmen Act, £200 000 was spent assisting 21 000 unemployed men to emigrate of whom over 13 000 were from London. In the 1920s there was a big increase in grants paid to the voluntary organizations involved in emigration schemes for the poor and the unemployed. By the late 1920s 350 000 had taken advantage of assisted passages, half of them going to Australia, one third to Canada and the rest to New Zealand. Many were lured by an extraordinary propaganda campaign waged by the Ministry of Labour and the Colonial Office which used posters in labour exchanges, magic-lantern shows and films to persuade the jobless that a better life awaited them on prairie farmsteads and in the Australian outback. To prepare them for a new life on the land the unemployed emigrants normally had to complete a training scheme on a farm colony like the Salvation Army's Hadleigh Colony in Essex. These six-week courses – heavily subsidized by the government – were similar in their military-style discipline to the work camps and had little practical value. But they played an important political role in attempting to convince the dominions that Britain was equipping them with useful skills and not simply dumping its most unskilled and unwanted citizens on them.

Labour exchanges also tried to attract unemployed men to go to Canada to help with the annual harvest when there was traditionally a big demand for unskilled labour. The rationale was that this would remove them from the dole, give them useful work discipline and perhaps lead to permanent emigration. A huge publicity drive in mining areas in 1928 led to 10 000 unemployed miners going over with assisted passages for the harvest. The

scheme however was badly organized and massively oversubscribed. Many discovered there were no jobs for them and quickly became destitute – they were shipped back home escorted by the police and the military.

From the late 1920s onwards there was a world agricultural depression and, with less demand for labour, Commonwealth countries drastically cut down on immigration. The government needed an alternative to colonial settlement. One possible solution to unemployment which aroused growing interest in the inter-war years was land settlement. Since the 1880s there had been small experiments in exporting unemployed men and their families from industrial to agricultural areas within Britain. Back-to-the-land idealists

**Men working at a Ministry of Labour Camp in the 1930s.
They were forced to go to the camps as part of the government's scheme
for the unemployed.**

believed that the countryside could provide a new and better life for the urban poor. The big increase in the jobless in the early 1930s brought a fresh government initiative to settle the long-term unemployed on the land. In 1934 the Land Settlement Association was formed. It purchased farms in different parts of the country and parcelled them up into smallholdings for vegetable, pig or poultry production. The new tenants became members of a farm cooperative which bought supplies, provided machinery and sold an array of agricultural produce from freshly laid eggs to tomatoes. There was hope that the scheme might in a small way begin to halt the long-term drift to the city which was depopulating the countryside.

The scheme was targeted at older long-term unemployed men aged between thirty-five and forty-five in 'distressed areas' who had little hope of future work. It was heavily promoted in the North-East where many Durham miners were recruited. If considered suitable the men were given a one-way ticket to the settlement, provided with a short training course and working capital of £130, then allotted a five-acre plot and a small modern cottage – which they had to help to build. They could then be joined by their families.

Around 3000 city dwellers embarked for the wilds of Newent in Gloucestershire, Sidlesham in Sussex, Fulney in Lincolnshire, and other more remote spots. But, for the majority, the dream of health and happiness amongst the shallots and runner beans never really materialized. The scheme was dogged by problems from the start. It proved to be fantastically expensive with the official start-up costs rising to more than £1000 per tenant, and it quickly became under-funded as the government withdrew funds. The training was inadequate and crops and animals were from time to time blighted with disease. There was only a small market for the goods the co-operatives produced and the tenants had to work round the clock just to survive. And, perhaps most damaging of all, many of the men and their families disliked the quietness and isolation of country life. Within two years most had returned to the towns and cities they had come from, happy to put up with periods of unemployment as long as they had the familiar cheap comforts of the pub, the chip shop and the picture palace to make life more bearable. A minority – often those with a passion for gardening who had lovingly cultivated their allotments back home – did stick it out, learnt by their mistakes and settled in the country. But by 1939 an official government report on the scheme had written it off as an expensive failure.

Most training schemes were aimed at men. Unemployment amongst women was of much less concern to the government, even though there were probably more women out of work than men in the depression years. A woman's place – especially a married woman – was ultimately seen to be in the

An unemployed man and his family pictured in Wigan in 1930. During the worst years of the depression there were almost four million out of work.

home. A marriage bar operated in most professions denying many married women the opportunity to work. Neither were they eligible for unemployment benefit. Consequently most women did not bother to register at labour exchanges. (This invisibility helped create the misleading official picture that the slump was hitting men harder than women.)

There were a few private initiatives to get women back to work. In 1935, for example, Lucy Clayton's model agency launched a scheme to bring 'attractive' young women languishing on the dole in South Wales to London to train as mannequins. This scheme was featured in a Paramount newsreel with a plummy, patronizing commentary describing how 'grooming is quite a new experience for them, giving to provincial girls a sophisticated West End beauty. The girls spend many hours in walking exercises as it is an important part of the mannequin's art to walk gracefully. These girls actually learn as quickly as girls brought up in easier surroundings.' The handful of women chosen for the two-week course were guaranteed a period of work with Miss Clayton's agency at £3 a week.

The main government scheme for unemployed women aimed to train them for domestic service and help solve the much aired 'servant problem'. Private service was traditionally the biggest employer of women and despite the advent of labour-saving devices in the new suburban middle-class home there were still over a million women working as domestics in the 1930s. But service was deeply unpopular amongst working-class women: the hours were long, the pay was pitiful, the status was low and the little free time enjoyed by live-in servants was often closely policed by employers. With growing opportunities for single women to work in offices, mills and new industries there was an increasing gap between supply and demand. The Ministry of Labour stepped in by offering 'homecraft courses' in most of 'the distressed areas' of South Wales, the North-East and Scotland where unemployment was highest. The courses lasted for thirteen weeks during which time the trainees were given instruction in cookery, table service, laundry work, cleaning, needlework and hygiene. By 1930 there were more than forty home-training centres, usually in converted private houses, including a number that specifically prepared girls for service in the Commonwealth and Empire which had their own servant problems. The daily regime was strict, preparing women for a subservient future. In some of the centres make-up was banned and trainees were chaperoned whenever they left the premises.

The insatiable demand for domestics meant that most graduates of these 'skivvy schools' had no problem in finding jobs. But the scheme was never successful in attracting large numbers of young women back into service. Even at its peak in the early 1930s only around 5000 a year were passing through the government home-training centres. One official survey of the 1930s found that of 30 000 women interviewed, two-thirds refused to even consider the possibility of entering service.

Another proposed solution to the continuing servant problem was to train unemployed men into private service. The Boy Scout movement made an extraordinary intervention in this area in the thirties with the Rover Scout Training and Employment Scheme. It proposed to train young, single unemployed men into parlourmen, kitchenmen, cooks, footmen, grooms, gardeners and chauffeurs. Five camps – run by 'Rover leaders' – were set up on country estates in Gloucestershire, Essex and Hampshire. The unemployed men were enrolled for training courses of three months which were particularly geared to the labour needs of the upper-class country house. Scout uniform was to be worn by the men during all their free time in the evenings and at weekends when they had to join in 'character-building activities' like general scouting, bridge-building, axemanship and boxing. Each was given two shillings and sixpence (12 new pence) a week pocket money and all were guaranteed a job at the end of the course. The Scouts boasted a 100 per cent placement rate of Rover trainees. Many, however, gave up their jobs after a few months or a few years – as did thousands of the officially trained female domestics – finding the low wages and the status hierarchies of the servant world intolerable.

There was a growing recognition in the inter-war years that unemployment was a fact of life and that government training schemes could only scratch the surface of such a deep-rooted problem. For some of those on the dole the experience of unemployment led to angry protest and politicization. Much of this protest was organized by the National Unemployed Workers Movement, formed in 1921 by Wal Hannington, an unemployed Communist engineer, with the aim of campaigning on behalf of the unemployed. At the peak of its activity in the early 1930s the NUWM claimed a membership of 50 000 unemployed men and women, many of whom were recruited from the (then) twice-weekly dole queues. NUWM members staged many demonstrations and protests – blocking Oxford Street with sit-downs, chaining themselves to the railings outside Downing Street, disrupting royal parades – in their battle to win national publicity for their campaign. They were also active on the government training schemes helping to articulate grievances and organizing strikes. The work camps were particular targets for

Police arrest a protestor at an unemployed demonstration near the House of Commons in January 1939.

disruption by NUWM 'infiltrators': Glenbranter, sixteen miles from Dunoon, had the 'worst' record of all with regular sit-downs and walk-outs staged by the unemployed men who had been sent there from Glasgow.

There was increasing official concern that the experience of long-term unemployment could destroy the politically quiescent and hard-working standards of traditional working-class behaviour. This prompted many attempts to fill the void of empty days on the dole and to help prop up the morale of unemployed men and their families. Most common were 'unemployed welfare centres', social clubs which encouraged the pursuit of every kind of useful hobby from table tennis to tailoring to choral singing. In the late 1930s these clubs claimed a membership of 200000. Many sporting activities were organized for the unemployed by labour exchanges. The London Area Unemployed Teams Cup Final was played at Wembley with the Prince of Wales there in the Royal Box to congratulate the players and present them with their medals. And in an age when an occasional holiday by the sea or in the countryside was beginning to be seen as the right of all city dwellers there were attempts by the authorities to provide free – or almost free – short breaks for the unemployed and their children. Unemployed men in London could for example enrol for a week at a bell-tented holiday camp in Nazeing in Essex to enjoy a rather regimented routine of swimming, exercises and country walks. And in Glasgow many children of the unemployed were eligible for summer 'Fresh Air Fortnights' in the countryside.

It was only with the arrival of war in 1939 that there was relief from the indignity and suffering of unemployment for the jobless and their families. Tragically, the waste of unemployment would be replaced by the waste of war. The expansion of war industries meant that by 1941 there were only 200000 people out of work and by 1943 unemployment had virtually ceased to exist. Britain had achieved full employment: for those who wanted to work there was plenty of it and those who didn't were forced to by law. So desperate was the labour shortage on the Home Front even hitherto marginalized groups – often hidden from the unemployment statistics – like married women and disabled people were recruited into war industries and essential services. For forty years the old mass-training schemes for the unemployed seemed to be a strange anachronism in British history that was quickly passing from living memory. But with the re-emergence of mass unemployment from the late 1970s onwards they have (in a new form) moved back onto the political agenda and into the lives of those without work.

WILL PHILPEN

In 1906 Will was born in Aberdare. His father had been a baker but became an alcoholic and in 1908 left his wife and son, taking Will's sister with him. Will did not see his sister again until he was twelve. In 1916 their father was killed fighting in the First World War. When he was thirteen Will left school and spent a year working on the pit top before being sent down the mine to work. He lost his job in 1926 after the General Strike.

After being unemployed for two years Will went on an assisted passage to Canada to work as a farm labourer. He returned to Wales after ten months and was sent on a training scheme in Bristol to learn how to become a cabinetmaker. In 1930 he started working down the mine again in South Wales. Will married later that year and has four children. He lives near Swansea.

"I had to walk twice a week to peg, you know, sign for the dole. When I got there this one week the hall was full of men and the manager got up on the stage and put up a huge poster. A beautiful scene of a bronzed farmer driving a team of horses through a field of golden corn, beautiful blue sky and a ball of fire, oh it was lovely d'you see? And it said underneath the poster three words: 'CANADA NEEDS YOU.' And the manager told us this tale, about how these farmers in Canada were expecting a bumper harvest and they needed workers. If we went we would be guaranteed five dollars a day. You would be met at Quebec by a representative and they would take you to a place of employment, everything would be fine.

I had no pictures at all. I knew nothing about Canada. I knew it was a country out there the other side of the world, a new country and that was all. So I decided, I had no job in Wales and no prospects of one. The adventure appealed to me and so did the money and this sounded ideal. I signed up for the scheme straight off.

It took us nine days to cross by ship, to reach Quebec and on the Sunday we arrived. We were met, I think, by the entire police force of Quebec. They stood shoulder-to-shoulder honest, they had revolvers which we had never seen in our lives you see and we had to march between them into a huge hangar, stood there about two hours. After that they had a special train and

**Young unemployed miners set off from Liverpool for Canada in 1928.
In that year ten thousand young men from mining areas were given assisted
passages to work on the Canadian harvest.**

there was two policemen on each step, still armed, and they stayed with us
until we reached the end of the province.

Winnipeg was fifteen hundred miles away and all they give us for that
journey was a small parcel, a bun, apple, one small tin of corned beef and a big
piece of cake and that was to last three days and two nights until we reached
Winnipeg. When we got there we were very hungry, believe me and thirsty, we
were all young men you see.

It was off the train again and into another huge hall and we were all told
to stand in front of these men with tables and books and it went like this. You

appeared before this clerk, he'd look at his book, 'Oh, four men wanted at so and so place, you and the next three. That's what we want…move on.' And my turn came and he looked at the book, 'Four men wanted at Mordern.' I didn't know where the hell Mordern was. 'Ah, you and the next three, see Mr Bradford when you get there.'

There were two men from Stoke and one Cockney, and me. So they gave us ten dollars for our train fare out and we reached Mordern about midday. Day like today, blue sky, beautiful sun. When we got there it was a typical prairie town: about eight wooden shacks, no roads or pavements, nothing, just simply … shacks put down on the prairie. A man stood there. I asked him where I could meet Mr Bradford. He laughed and said, 'There's no such man. You've been had lad, he doesn't exist.' And then we knew, we'd been conned see.

We were broke, we had no money, no job. It was flat for three hundred mile, dirty, brown, burnt by the sun, the prairie. It's a lousy, miserable place, nothing, no green, no trees, terrible. We didn't know what to do. So we sat in the shade and waited… About six o'clock an old car, falling to pieces, pulled up, it was filthy and the farmer even filthier and he wanted one man. The Cockney jumped in and we never saw him again. Then later on another man called Bill Stewart came in and he wanted all three of us. He wanted us for what they called 'stooking' that is gather the wheat up, the sheaves in bundles of rows so they could drive the wagon between them see. We would be working about eighteen hours a day and we would get sixteen shillings a day.

It was murder, believe me. I was used to working on the coal face, I thought that was hard but it was child's play compared to this. We had to get up, we had to take a lantern, clean out the horses, feed them, water them and wash our hands, nobody bothered about washing your faces there, then go in and have some food. We were very well-fed, well they had to feed you because you was working so hard and we were healthy young men. Then we used to drive out to the fields and the thrasher. You had to keep strictly to your turn, keep working and if you didn't you was paid off you see, on the spot, and 'twas backbreaking. It was a hundred in the shade and very often we were drenched in sweat.

It was murder, absolute murder and we had to keep going from five in the morning until one o'clock. Then we had a one-hour drive back to the farm, see to the horses first because the horses were very important, far more important than we were, we were nothing, dirt you see. P'raps you had time for a quick smoke and hitch up again and off until nine o'clock at night. You weren't allowed any time off. If you didn't load the wagon full and get back in time you were given your cards. No union out there. We were exhausted. I used to go back to the farm, see to the horses, go in and have food, climb up the ladder an' drop in the hay, gone sound asleep. Did that seven days a week. I don't know how we stuck it.

I was always thinking of home, I wanted to get back home but I knew that I had to get the money to get back and so I did everything I could to get every penny.

We were on the farm for three weeks thrashing and then it finished. I found out about an outfit ten miles away, a farm that was one man short. I was desperate to earn money so I went over there to work for this farmer Anderson and his wife. But they were not pleasant people. When I first arrived they didn't speak to me. He gave me a lantern and told me to get up in the loft, there was no hay there, I just lay all night. He came up in the morning about four o'clock and told me to clean the stables out. He asked me if I could drive and I said I could although I'd never driven in my life. But I jumped on the wagon and I got along OK with it.

But I was always hungry there and I used to go into the barn in where the chickens were and steal the eggs, suck them about half a dozen at a time. A desperate man will do things that he wouldn't normally do you see. You're not going to lay down and starve, I wouldn't, no bloody fear.

I was there about two months working seven days a week and I finished up anyway with about three hundred dollars in my belt and that was a hell of a lot of money then believe me. That's the only thing that kept me going, the thought of getting this money to get myself out of there.

In the finish I had to walk fifteen miles to the nearest little town across the prairie. Then I caught the train back to Winnipeg. It was a big city, skyscrapers and all that and things I'd never seen before.

I went into this little pool-room and I was sat there watching a chap opposite, obviously like me, one of the harvesters and he came over and we decided between us to join up. We looked for digs, I remember it quite well, six dollars a night, nothing to eat, and we were there a week. I sent half my money home to me mother because my stepfather was still on the dole and in the night we had a few fags and a few pints – enjoyed it.

Then we tried to get to work, impossible. We couldn't even afford to sleep in the digs. We had to pack it up and go sleep in the railway station on a bench. One night while we was at the station we saw an advert in a newspaper,

'Men wanted up in Invermey'. We counted our money and we had just enough between us to get there so we went, travelled all night. We got there in the morning, just a little one-horse town about a dozen buildings, no more and they told us, 'No, no work here'. We'd been conned again you see, we were stuck. We were desperate, we had no money, no work, no prospect of work, we knew that we'd been had. We were the only ones that got off that train. That's right, no one else. Dead absolutely dead. But nothing we could do nothing at all, we had to accept it, we had to, well, you had to fight for yourself then.

After sitting there for about an hour a motorbike arrived, one of the Mounties, and he said, 'I'm sorry but it's the law here if you haven't got any money or a job and no one to stand for you you automatically go to prison for six months.' It was what they called the Vagrancy Act. So we started walking down the railroad and he stood and watched us till we were out of sight.

A few miles down the line one man we met, he said to ride the freight. 'Just make sure that you don't let 'em see you get on, keep out of sight.'

There was a train just along the tracks, sixty wagons all there waiting so when they started hitching up we crept out quietly and climbed up which was very difficult. There's a catwalk on top of Canadian trains, about six inches higher, so we stuck our cases there and we laid down there.

Just before the train started off a light came along and the guard was walking along the top of the catwalk going to the engine see. We thought he was going to throw us off but he stopped and spoke to us, decent chap, we were lucky. He just let us stay there.

So the train starts. We were absolutely terrified. It was bustling along about sixty miles an hour because it's flat open air, no bridges just three locomotives chasing along and we were lying gripping onto the top of the wagon and 'twas freezing cold. We pushed our arms underneath the catwalk and our faces on the plank and we worked our feet along underneath until we were literally frozen to the plank. We were afraid of being thrown off 'cos the train was belting along you see. We were absolutely terrified and it wasn't till hours later that we saw the smoke of Quebec.

To think we were suffering so much. And our clothes, well, we were stinking, we had nowhere to go, it was a big city and we were sleeping in doorways. We were starving and so my mate said, 'I don't care a damn if they put me in prison, I've got to have food.' And we went into a shop and we ordered food but we didn't have it because when we went in the man phoned for the police and in about two minutes he closed the shop and the police came and took us to a lock-up prison and we was there for four days. But we were fed at least.

At the end of our time in prison, we were told that we were being sent home, to Wales. And the police escorted us all the way to the port, more or less frog-marched us onto the ships, we were back in Wales in nine days. I think the Canadian people were glad to see the back of us, they were so alarmed, you see, there were about ten thousand of us in all and we were a danger to them, we were starving and we weren't going to lie down and starve no way."

KATE REYNOLDS

Kate was born in 1892 in Old Pelton, County Durham, one of a family of eleven. Her father was a master check weighman dealing with the cargo on the docks. In 1919 Kate met and married her husband, a miner. They had four children. In 1926 after the General Strike Kate's husband lost his job and was unemployed for three years until the family were offered a place on the Land Settlement Scheme. They moved to their smallholding in Andover in November 1936 and worked there for the next twelve years. Kate's husband then went to work as a batman for the air force. They never moved back to the North-East and Kate still lives in Andover.

"It was cold weather when we came down and the warden came and met us and brought us out to the house. They couldn't get the furniture van up because the roads were so bad, had to bring it over the fields. We had to climb up the bankside to get up to the house 'cos there was no steps up into the front door.

Well, I set to and I wallpapered the sitting-room, the bedroom and tried to make the best of the house. And me husband was digging the cesspit outside. We both had to go then and dig out the piggeries and we did it our two selves. He used to fill the bucket, I used to carry it and put it in a barrow up on a little hill and then wheel it away. Well, after that we had to start and build the huts for the poultry.

Kate Reynolds and her daughter-in-law photographed with the family's pet pig, Betty, on their small holding in Andover in 1940.

Very hard work, you had to be on the go at half-past seven in the morning, the cockerel used to let you know that, till it got dark at night. Always something to do, to clean out, to feed, eggs to gather, and to see the rats wasn't there. We always used to have the dogs there to watch over the rats.

We had two goats and one duck and four pens of chickens, oldish hens. One night a weasel got in and killed one whole ark full of birds. Then there was two lots of pigs and when they had little ones, the piglets, we had them on harness so they could roam right around their pen. Well that manured the ground and that used to be handy when my husband had to dig the place. I looked after them pigs but he used to clean it out, we used to help each other.

You really got very attached to those animals. That Betty, one pig that we had, she was a proper pet and she used to lie down and I used to sit on her. Well I used to say she talked to us and I would, you know, rub her tummy and I would say, 'Now what about yer leg, d'you want yer leg rubbed?' And 'twould lift up its leg for us to rub and it would be grunting along.

But in the end we was meant to take them to market, to get our money. We had this nanny-goat, well she was a pet, we had her from a baby. And when her time came my son, he was sittin' and crying his eyes out. It made you feel like that 'cos we didn't like to do away with them but we all had to do the same. They were just like children, you didn't like parting with them. One of the ducks, Donald, we let it run round, we wouldn't kill it.

We used to grow beautiful cauliflowers and that, the brussels sprouts. We grew the melons, cucumbers and marrows as well as all the rest of the vegetables. We tried outdoor tomatoes but they were a failure 'cos they used to get potato blight. Then we started doing it in the winter. We got the glasshouse which was my husband's favourite, he liked being amongst the soil and we set it up with fifteen hundred tomato plants. We used to have to stoke to get the heat through in the glasshouse, to get the plants to grow.

We had to put all our produce in through the farm and the price when it came back of course, the settlement took their share out before we got ours, the cream off. And they bought all the seeds and stuff in wholesale and we had to pay the full price off them.

You had to help each other, 'twas no use a man trying to do it hisself, he had to have help and all the women used to do the same. We all mucked in together until everything was done. But it was our life and 'twas our livelihood and we made the best of it. It was up to you whether you made it good or bad. We were quite content to be in our own home with our family, so once you got your animals all bedded down for the night and saw that your glasshouses and that were all put right, well we used to be cosy indoors with our lanterns.

One day a big car turned up, big Cadillac, great big fur coat rug inside and it was one of the heads on the settlement committee. He got out and he had the nerve to ask my husband could we not make more money as they weren't gettin' nothin' much out of it. How did we expect him to live? So of course my husband turned around and said we'd kept such as him long enough and we wasn't going to keep 'em no longer. I knew then that we were finished and 'twas what we wanted. We'd done our share and we'd done all what they'd asked us to do, we couldn't do no more, could we?"

BEN RUSS

Ben was born in Swansea in 1918, the youngest of two sons. His father worked as a cleaner on the buses and his mother was a tin-cutter in the local steel works. At the age of fourteen Ben started working at the same works as his mother cutting tin plate. When he reached the age of sixteen and he should have been paid a full wage, Ben was sacked. He was unemployed for two years.

In 1933 the labour exchange sent him to Brechfa Labour Camp for three months where he worked on the stone quarries. After he returned from Brechfa there was still no suitable employment and so Ben joined the army. He was in the army for fifteen years and then worked underground in the collieries for fourteen years. After a pit accident Ben left the colliery and went to work in a plastics factory. Ben married his childhood sweetheart in 1941 and they had three children. They live in Swansea.

"I had a job in the tin works and when we got about sixteen or seventeen I asked for some more money so they made an excuse for to get rid of me, they sacked me. They didn't want to give me more money.

Well I never had no money then 'cos me father had to keep me and his wages was small. And I was courting too. My girlfriend asked me one night if I'd go to the pictures and so I went and asked me mother for a sixpence. She said, 'I haven't got sixpence, do you think I'm made of money?' So I picked up the stool and I smacked it on the table and I broke a couple of dishes. My mother turned round and smacked my face for me. Well, I wanted to be able to treat me girlfriend like and I stole sixpence out me mother's purse. She found out of course, I knew she would, and she guessed it were me, she never forgave me for that. I felt terrible 'cos things were so bad, money was so tight, you couldn't do nothing.

I went down the labour exchange for to sign on and they said there was a camp set up for the unemployed, they sent you there for to 'arden you, for to get you used to working pick-and-shovel quarry work, forestry. I'd have to go for a few months, no choice, either I went or I lost me dole. I'd go to the camp, work in the stone quarry and get two shillings and ten Woodbines a week.

They sent me the train ticket, get the train to Carmarthen, then we all had to get on these lorries, me and about a hundred other men. 'God almighty,'

Men breaking stones at a 'slave camp' in the 1930s. After their three-month stint of hard labour and military-style discipline, most men returned to the dole queues.

I said, 'we're going to hell and back.' It was bloody miles out. There was nothing there at all, only like fields and woods and the river, nothing at all.

When we got to the camp, this fella came out, they called him the Major, he had these britches on and a hat and a stick. In his hands he had a pair of brown leather gloves and he was banging these against his thigh like. He said, 'You're here to work, not bloody shirk and work you will.'

We was shown these huts where we had to sleep. There was no showers, just bowls of water. The only toilets that was in the camp was down the bottom of the field with a big hole cut in the ground and seats put on 'em with a tin sheet covering the top.

And the food from breakfast to dinner-time was all bloody corned beef sandwiches. The staff, them buggers used to have bacon and eggs for breakfast of a bloody morning and we had porridge, like a lump of bloody mud slapped on yer plate, no milk with it.

Some of the boys was bloody starving and they used to say, 'Let's go down and catch a bloody rabbit and cook the bugger.' One time the boys caught a rabbit, skinned him through and cooked 'im on an open stove you know. Went down the next day and only half the bloody rabbit was there, a fox or a badger must have pinched the rabbit.

We were doled out clothes to wear for to work in. I had to stuff paper up the toes of the boots to make them fit my feet, you know, and two cotton shirts with little patches on and then you had a wet suit, oilskins for the legs and a sou'wester.

It was January and we had snow and down the quarry it was very cold so I got fed up and I put me waterproof on. The ganger came out and said, 'What's wrong with you? You bloody cold?' And he wouldn't let me work with me coat on, 'Keep working you'll get warm,' he said. Slogging, bloody sledge-hammer.

So I was slogging away with the old sledge-hammer. Me hands were full of blisters and this old chap there told me to pee on my hands and make them tough. So I done it and it bloody stung, burned but after that the skin came all hard and so they didn't trouble me as much.

This ganger you know he had a white-handled pick shaft and wherever he went he kept tapping it on the ground as much to say, 'You start any nonsense and I'll belt you with it.' He made sure he was in charge, he even told us when we could stop. 'You can have a smoke now. Ten minutes then back to work.'

Ben Russ and his wife Kitty photographed in 1940.

You dared not smoke till he blew that whistle. Lit the fag and everybody would have a whiff and when you'd smoked half he'd say, 'Right, fags out.' Then he'd come round and count nine and a half cigarettes, anybody only had eight then he stopped your allowance. He caught me one time with an extra cigarette and I told him it was the tobacco that me father had sent me. 'Your Woodbines are stopped,' he said but all the boys ganged up, got onto him and said, 'If you stop his Woodbines then we'll push you through the stone crusher.' And believe me they really meant it. We'd have done jail for him. That's the state most of the men were in. Most of them wanted a bloody riot.

In a way we were just bloody rubbish because of the way they treated us. It was proper slavery for two bob a week, ten Woodbines and a three ha'penny stamp, very hard. Even I've seen men crying, not because it was hard work because some of those men were ex-colliery men, they knew what hard work was. They was crying because of the bloody camp.

Then one day it all got to me, I got a little bit fed up and I went down the field and I started to cry and an old fella came up to me and asked me what's the matter. 'You know,' he said, 'it takes a bloody man to cry.'

There was nothing else other than work, slogging all day long and by the time you got to yer bed then you was straight out to sleep, you were that tired.

The only sport we got was Saturdays. To have a game we used to have a newspaper and soak it wet, squeeze all the water out then put a sack round it and tie it and have a game of rugby. Some of them boys up the valley were rough buggers you know they used to push you, half strangle you.

When it got to the night-time you couldn't go anywhere, used to sit on the bed and light the old oil lamps, two hurricane lamps and if we had enough coke we'd keep a fire going. One night one of the old fellas said everybody had to sing a song or else put a cigarette in the box. So I started to sing this song:

> Send me a letter, send it by mail,
> Send it in care of Brechfa jail,
> I'm in the jailhouse, down on my knees,
> Praying for heaven, for my release.

When I got home after me three months was up I went down the labour exchange again to sign on. After a couple of weeks this fella behind the counter, short fella with thick pebble glasses said, 'Oh yes, got a job for you Mr Russ, up London,' he says. Selling Eldorado ice-cream in a bloody wheelbarrow thirty bob a week. I said, 'Hell, I've just come back from Brechfa man, I wants a decent job man in Swansea, near.' He told me me dole was stopped and he pointed his finger at me and he said, 'Join the bloody army.' I went to grab 'old of him and me mate said to me, 'Taff, don't bloody touch him, he's only got to press a button and your feet won't touch the ground, you'll be in the nick.' So I just stepped backwards and I walked out.

There wasn't much I could do, and I thought that the army couldn't be much worse than Brechfa so I went to join up."

MAY ROGERS

May was born in 1918 in South Shields. Her mother died later that year leaving her husband, a railwayman, to look after their two children. Their father remarried and May was brought up with her brother and two step-sisters. When she was fourteen May left school and started work at a biscuit factory. However, the job did not last long and in 1935, after being unemployed for several months May was sent to a training school for domestic servants by the labour exchange. After her year's training she was sent to work for a wealthy family as a maid in their house in Harrogate. She worked there for four years until she met and married her husband in 1939. They have three children and still live together in Harrogate.

"It was very hard to get a job. I'd got to about sixteen and me father and mother were fed up with me because I was eating and being clothed but I wasn't bringing any money in, you see. So I went and told them at the labour exchange and they asked me if I wanted to go to a school where I could learn how to be a domestic. There was one condition attached to it, you had to take a job afterwards in a town away from home. Well, I wanted to get away and do something so I decided that I'd better start at this school.

It was in this big Victorian house with two teachers. They were very stern with you, you know, kept you in order. We had to learn all about domestic science, we had to wash and cook and clean. And we had all these nice silver candlesticks and brass moneyboxes and all that to clean. The meals that we cooked, we had them for our lunch and we all had to learn how to serve at the table. And we had to make our own uniforms, it was all done by hand. We had

**May Rogers in 1937 at the house in Harrogate where she worked
as a maid for four years.**

to learn how to answer the door and the telephone. We couldn't do it
sometimes for giggling you know. And they told us about the better side of the
job, flower arranging in the rooms and that.

At the end of our training they gave us the jobs, there was no choice. But
oh, I had high hopes. I thought I might go to a private house where there were
other maids, or a hotel even. And they said if we stayed in our jobs for nine
months we could write away to the school and they would send us a badge, like
a shield, gold and black. I stayed four years actually.

Me mother put me on the train and someone met me at the other end and we went straight down to where me employer was. The lady of the house says, 'I'll take you up and show you your room first and then we'll talk over your duties.' She stopped at an attic and opened the door. I thought, 'Oh, I wish I'd never come, of all the places to put a young girl a damned attic up among the birds.'

I felt really unhappy the first week. I couldn't stop crying. I was so lonely, you couldn't make friends see – I was the only maid in that house.

You were treated as a general maid, dogsbody. I mean there were no need for all that work you know. You could have finished roughly about five o'clock like a proper job but she was looking for jobs for me to do, she wouldn't have me sitting idle. She used to go round and see if I'd done all the dusting and she'd chastise me if I'd missed this out or missed that out. She wouldn't let me have any privacy, she even used to search me room. It was the lowest kind of job there is. I was overworked and underpaid and starving half the time. I even took some meat, just a few left-overs from the kitchen one time and I got ever so told off about that.

I really put hard work into that school you know to be somebody. I was really blazing mad, all those days training I did for this job, to be degraded and work like a slave.

In fact after a year I wrote home and asked me mother and father could I come back home. But they said it was my idea, going away from home and that I could stay away now. So I had to put up with it.

I really was unhappy but after about the second year I just got acclimatized to it, I had no choice. I just didn't care anymore and I just kept thinking, 'Well, I'll be here till I'm an old maid.' No way could I get out of it. If she found out I were looking for another job she would have sacked me on the spot so I just laboured on and on.

It was lucky I met me husband. One evening we stood talking outside the gate after ten o'clock. The lady of the house came down the garden path and played hell with us because I was supposed to be in by ten. Well, me husband turned round and he says to her, 'Well she's leaving, this is the last week, she's going to work for you 'cos she's going to marry me, I'm taking her away from you. You've done nothing but keep her as a slave.'

So that is just what we did. I worked out the week and then I left and we got married as soon as we could. I would never have taken the job in the first place if I'd have known it were going to be general dogsbody. I felt as if I'd served a sentence when I left that place, I felt free."

TOM DURKIN

Tom, born in 1915, was brought up with his three brothers and five sisters in Ballinrobe in the west of Ireland. Their father was a carter and small-time farmer. At the age of thirteen Tom was expelled from school for fighting with the schoolmaster. He couldn't find permanent employment in Ireland and so in 1933 he left for Sheffield where he stayed for a short time with some relations. Tom then began his search for work in the north of England, walking from town to town. Although he worked on and off as a casual labourer on building-sites, for the majority of the next six years he was without a job.

In 1936 Tom joined the National Unemployed Workers Movement and started to get actively involved in the campaign against unemployment. In 1938 he joined the Communist Party. It wasn't until the Second World War in 1939 that Tom was employed full-time in the building industry, working on preparations for the feared invasion and rebuilding bomb-damaged sites. In 1940 he married and went on to have three children. The family settled in Willesden, north-west London, where Tom and his wife still live. After the war ended Tom continued to work in the construction industry. He has been very active in the trade union movement and was a founder member of CND in 1956. Tom still works for a number of Trade Union councils, as well as being a delegate of the south-east region of the TUC.

"There were illusions about the promised land somewhere, either America, Canada, England, Australia, New Zealand. If you were a fit, strong young person there'd be something wrong with you if you didn't migrate. It was the done thing.

The village blacksmith he used to say to us youngsters, 'You should go to Sheffield, that's where all the work is.' I fell for this and I decided to go.

Of course I got a terrific shock. You go out of an environment that's green, a vast panoramic view stretching for miles to the Connemara mountains. You go into a city and nobody seems to know anyone else, all the houses are on top of one another. All the factories practically were closed down, you can see all the chimneys, there's no smoke. I went out of the frying-pan not into the fire but into a furnace.

I didn't know what to do, you see you couldn't get dole and I had no money. I was staying with a relative and I didn't want to be a parasite on them. I hung around for a little while, I thought to myself, 'God, what have I got myself into?'

After a bit I got a job on a building-site but there was a strong kind of nationalism, if there were any jobs going Sheffield natives should have them. Foreigners were not very welcome to say the least. The foreman gave me twice as much work as anyone else, it was slavery, no breaks at all. A boy would come round with a pail of tea, you dipped your cup into this bucket but you drank while you were working. It was pick and shovel all day long. My hands were beginning to get blisters and the sun was beating down. He kept on saying, 'Come on, you bloody Irish coming over here.' I only lasted a day and a half and he sacked me.

I began to feel that I wish I had wings to fly off again back to where I came from, die there rather than die here. I had no home so I thought, 'Well, I'll take to the road, I won't be a parasite.' That was when I went on the tramp looking for work. You began to share experiences, there were so many people on the road, every mile or so. 'Where are you going?' 'Oh, we've just come from there, there's no jobs there.' They'd tell you where there might be a good place for a kip for the night. And then I began to feel, 'Well, I'm not alone.'

You got cold and wet but you just kept walking until your body heat dried it out. I mean when the sun is shining on a summer day and you're walking along the road, alongside the woods, fields with animals in it, it's not so bad, there's nobody pushing you and you think, 'I can survive I can, I can get on even in this life the way it is, and maybe sooner or later then I'll get a job and something better'll come along.'

I started to walk to Preston because I'd been told that they were building a big factory there and needed men. That took me about four months, and I slept on the side of the road mostly 'cos the weather was getting fine. You lay yourself down under a hedge, at the side of a field. All kinds of living things would begin to come out at night, rats and mice and voles, make a noise, rustling all the time. I used to have strange thoughts. I remember one night I was sleeping, it was a beautiful starry night, the sky was just dotted, absolutely clear, and I was thinking to myself, 'I wonder if out there in all this vast space there's other poor creatures like us, you know, that are tramping round on some other planet.' You begin to wonder about life and about nature and what it's all about.

After walking all the way to Preston I couldn't get a job there without you bribed the foreman. All I could get was some work on a nearby site and it was too dangerous, it was deep trenches and there was no proper timber and support. It could close in at any time and I said, 'No, I'm not going to work here, we're not ready to die yet.'

You would get depressed. You might go into a place where there'd be a library, have a look at the papers, see all the bad news from round the world, unemployment, depression. I couldn't see any hope, you know. I didn't understand much about the causes of unemployment at the time but I used to hear from people I would meet on the road about hunger marches coming down from the north and the campaign against unemployment.

See, round the country at the time there were marches, hunger marches, and I became interested. So when I turned up in London, of course, I found it very difficult to get a job. There were some people that I grew up with, eleven people in this tenement, nine unemployed, two working, it was in Edgware Road so I holed up there.

I signed on and often outside the labour exchange speakers from the National Unemployed Workers Movement would turn up and they'd make a speech. There was eight thousand signing on, there'd be great big queues with police in between them so it was an ideal place, they had a captive audience. They gave you leaflets and they said there'd be a march, there'd be a demonstration, and then it became a topic of conversation. I began to go to some meetings and hear speakers like Wally Hannington.

We planned various protests. We would walk into places like the Dorchester carrying plates with us, we'd go inside, walk in where the rich people were dining and begin to agitate and create. I went to Cambridge Circus. We got tickets and went into this show and then in the interval the piano would come up, and that was our opportunity to get on the stage and get out our posters, 'We Want Jobs'. The people in general they wouldn't be hostile and the management wouldn't like to manhandle you, to throw you out.

I chained myself to railings with a number of others at Hammersmith because there was an unemployed march coming in at the time from Wales.

A protest by the unemployed in London's Oxford Street in 1938.
The NUWM staged many such demonstrations to gain national publicity for their campaign.

DO YOUR OWN THINKING

The Man Underneath: "I'm just thinking what would happen if I were to stand up?"

PLEBS LEAGUE, 162a Buckingham Palace Road, LONDON — S.W.1   2d

They were mainly miners and some of us then chained ourselves to railings saying, you know, 'We want jobs and we are slaves. We have no future.' It was all just to get publicity for the unemployed.

The police would be there to drag you away but you could hold the traffic up or do enormous dislocation, and everyone was saying, 'What's all this about?' You caused people to talk and people'd say, 'Oh there's these poor unemployed.'

There was nothing much the police could do only maybe give you a cuff round the ear or tell you to get off or threaten you. Not much good fining you, you had no money. I was often involved and chased and threatened and they might thump you a bit.

I was in Birmingham when the coronation was on. The people weren't, you know, all elated over the coronation, especially ordinary working people because they'd all the problems to contend with, and they could see that a lot of this was just wasting money. You know, keep the people a bit quiet, give them bread and circuses. We in the NUWM had a sort of counter demonstration. We had posters and we were shouting out things like, 'Money for jobs not royal junketing'. And of course that was regarded as an insult to the royal family, the worst thing of all you could do.

The police come along and they started shifting us away, they got rough and give us a fierce beating but we kept shouting, 'Why don't we use the money for the unemployed and people who are destitute?' We all got arrested and taken to the police station. When they took me into the cell there was two big cops had hold of me and I said, 'I'm not drunk and I want a doctor to examine me to prove it.' So one looks and says, 'All right then, I'll get you a doctor.' So he goes outside and brings in two other cops and one of them caught me by each arm and pulled me round and the other one started punching me into the face, he cut me to pieces. When they took me up to the court they didn't let me wash meself, me hair was wild and me face there was blood on it. I was charged with creating a breach of the peace and that I was very violent and that I attacked a policeman. The old magistrate on the bench was reading the riot act to me and so I was very lucky because I only got a fortnight in Winston Green Prison."

A pamphlet produced by The Plebs League in the 1930s as part of their series *Books For Workers*. The Plebs League was an organization connected with the National Council of Labour Colleges.

5

VOICES IN
THE DARK
SEXUAL ABUSE

In 1909 an NSPCC inspector in Stockton was called in to investigate an alleged case of 'child neglect and carnal knowledge'. The case involved eleven-year-old Emily Wilson, the daughter of a poverty-stricken casual labourer, the father of four children. Her mother had died in 1900 and Emily shared the same bed as her father. Emily's seventeen-year-old brother also lived in their two-roomed home. The complaint of neglecting Emily appeared to the inspector to be well-founded. 'I examined her, she was filthy with head and body vermin, black with dirt. The clothing were old worn-out rags.' The inspector investigated the alleged incestuous relationship by interviewing Emily.

"I asked the little girl if she went on all right. She said yes, 'me dad takes me to the "Grand" and to the "pictures" and "Hippodrome" but he will not buy me any more clothes and boots and I don't like sleeping with him because he hurts me in bed.' She said he lay on his back and then set her on top of him and pushed his thing against her thing. She said, 'he used to do it to my sister but she went away and then he started to do it to me. He did it on Monday night and three times last week. It always makes him sick and bad next morning. It makes me feel bad too and gives me stomach-ache. I do not cry much I am too much out of breath and he says if I tell anyone he will hit me and not take me to the "Grand". I have only told my sister and she said she would tell you (the inspector). Did she send you?' I told her yes and that she was a good girl to tell me about it. I asked her if her brother knew and she said no. I asked her if he heard her cry and she said she did not cry a big row. I asked her if her brother ever slept with her and she said not for a long time

now. I asked if anyone else hurt her. She said, she would not let anyone else do to her what her father does in bed. She would kick them and tell her father."

At the request of the inspector Emily was medically examined a few days later by a doctor, who wrote in his report:

"I found a slight soreness of the external genitals and that the hymen was absent but otherwise there were no marks of violence. There were no lacerations at the entry to the vagina nor was the passage dilated as one would have expected if complete connection had taken place. I am therefore unable from my examination to confirm the child's story."

The doctor did however confirm the fact that Emily was severely neglected by her father and she was on his recommendation removed to a children's home. Her father was not prosecuted for incest.

This is one of the few cases of child sexual abuse that was documented in any detail during the first half of the century. In an age before widespread state intervention into family life the NSPCC was the main agency that dealt with allegations of parental mistreatment of children. Around the turn of the century it drew attention to the hidden problem of child sexual abuse and campaigned for the passage of the 1908 Punishment of Incest Act which criminalized incest for the first time in British history. But even after the legislation there was only a handful of prosecutions for incest each year. By 1914 the recognition of child sexual abuse virtually disappeared from NSPCC records and from public view. The vast majority of prosecutions of parents continued to be made on the grounds of neglect. This was essentially because it was much more simple to prove 'neglect' while evidence for 'sexual abuse' was far more difficult to establish – as is vividly illustrated in the case of Emily Wilson. By the 1920s the NSPCC was dealing with more than 50 000 cases of suspected neglect and cruelty to children each year. What proportion of these were in fact incest cases we will never know, but there seems little doubt that sexual abuse was far more widespread than was ever officially recognized.*

The personal testimony of older people who were abused as children gives us a clue to the extent of sexual abuse in the past. Their memories also provide a

* This description of child sexual abuse in Cleveland draws heavily on Harry Ferguson's unpublished Ph.D. thesis, 'Protecting Children in Time' (Trinity College, Dublin, 1993).

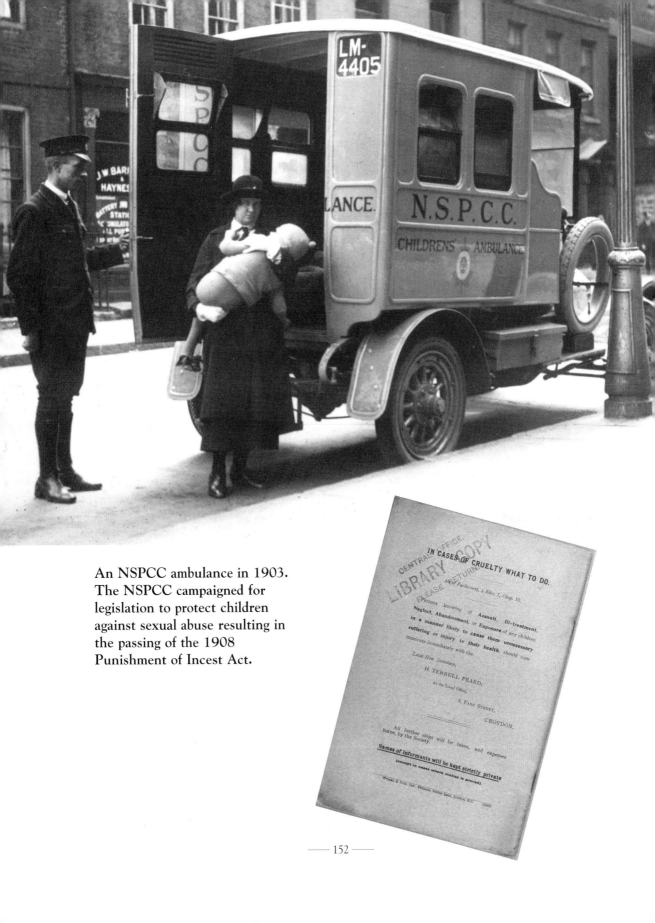

An NSPCC ambulance in 1903. The NSPCC campaigned for legislation to protect children against sexual abuse resulting in the passing of the 1908 Punishment of Incest Act.

graphic picture of who the abusers were and of the relationships between the abusers and the abused. In our research we have corresponded with or interviewed 120 survivors of sexual abuse. They contacted us through letters that we placed in local newspapers all over Britain asking for memories of child sexual abuse during the first half of the century. Of these victims, the vast majority of them had not reported the abuse at the time. In fact in almost two-thirds of the cases, we were the first people they had ever spoken to about their experience.

Those who contacted us ranged from forty-five to eighty-five years of age. They came from a variety of backgrounds suggesting that incest was not a problem restricted to the 'rough' working-classes as was often thought at the time. In many cases the abuse took place in what on the surface appeared to be very ordinary, respectable families. More than three-quarters of those who wrote to us were women. The incestuous relationships were predominantly heterosexual and in all but three cases the abusers were male. In the majority of cases the abuse took place within the family and the abuser was the father. Stepfathers, elder brothers, step-brothers, uncles and grandfathers were also involved in abuse, though to a far lesser extent.

Slightly less than a quarter of all the experiences of abuse described to us occurred outside the family. Of these most were committed by strangers, but there was a significant minority of abuse by priests, teachers and carers in institutions. Most sexual abuse of boys seems to have been of this sort, committed by men who weren't part of the family and who were often in a strong position of moral authority and control over the child. For example, all the five people we spoke to who were abused as children by priests were men.

In a few cases the abuse seems to have begun when the child was a toddler – some of the first memories are of sexual interference by the father. Most commonly, however, the abuse began between the ages of five to eight. It frequently continued for several years. In cases of incest 90 per cent of those we interviewed recalled that the sexual relationship lasted for more than a year. In a number of instances it carried on for several years into and beyond adolescence. The abuse was remembered as occurring very frequently. Most believed it had happened at least once a week and for some it was a nightmare that had to be endured every day.

With young children the abuse normally took the form of masturbation – the child would masturbate the adult. Oral sex and the pushing of objects inside the anus and the vagina were also common. As the child got older, penetration and full sexual intercourse often occurred on a regular basis. In some cases

A publicity photograph from the 1919 film *Broken Blossoms*. This was one of the few films of the time to portray a violent father's relationship with his daughter.

where there was a family history of incest, there was collusion with other members of the family who would also be invited to have sex with the child. In a few cases the abuse was also accompanied by torture and extreme violence.

The abusers used a combination of bribes and punishments to get what they wanted. Sweets and small gifts were sometimes given in the early stages of the abuse. These could be of immense significance to poor children who were cold and hungry, and who rarely enjoyed any treats. There also might be a special show of tenderness for the abused child. In families where there was little love and affection this could give a father immense influence over his young daughter. But most important in the incest relationship was punishment or the threat of punishment. More than half of those we have interviewed described their fathers or abusers as violent characters of whom they were frightened. In many cases they hit their wives and their children. Most daughters learned through experience that if they did not comply with their father's wishes they would be punished or all love for them would be withdrawn.

Most children had little concept of resisting the abuse. They were brought up in families where there was a 'seen and not heard' attitude to children in which they were expected to do as they were told. Stern Victorian attitudes of 'spare the rod, spoil the child' were still widespread during the first half of this century, but they were particularly characteristic of families in which there were incestuous relationships. In these families, when father was at home his word was law and there was no room for questioning his decisions. In this authoritarian atmosphere the 'good' daughter obeyed her father's will. In most cases she quietly endured the abuse for long periods and submitted to her father's demand that she should not tell anyone of their 'little secret'.

But there was some resistance from the young victims of incest. The abuse was painful and frightening, and they wanted it to stop. Most children also had a strong feeling that there was something fundamentally wrong with what they were being told to do. In the majority of cases resistance took the form of telling the mother, an older sister or a sympathetic relative or adult about the abuse. This was often very difficult and traumatic for the child as any talk about sex was still taboo in most families and the children had no vocabulary to express what had happened to them.

In all the cases we have come across the abuser denied the accusation. Where the mother was very weak, ill or completely dominated by the father, she often did nothing to protect her daughter and the incest continued much as before. In a few cases there was probably collusion between the parents with the mother turning a blind eye to the abuse, wishing her daughter to perform unwanted sexual duties. In these circumstances the only hope for the abused daughter was to run away and leave home for good – which some did. However, in most cases when the mother was told about the abuse it stopped. Although the father invariably denied the charge, he was too frightened to continue and the mother was more vigilant in protecting her daughter. Even when the child's story was believed it was extremely rare for it to be reported to a doctor or to the police. Most families seemed to have wanted to avoid the stigma of any publicity and the added financial hardship that would have resulted from the breadwinner being fined or imprisoned. The handful of cases that were reported were invariably dismissed on the grounds of insufficient evidence. None of the abusers of the 120 survivors of child sexual abuse spoken to were prosecuted.

The abuse had a devastating effect on the lives of most of those who contacted us. Many became withdrawn as children, they suffered from depression and were prone to eating disorders. Around a quarter felt suicidal or in some cases attempted suicide as young women. Most experienced serious problems forming lasting relationships as adults and in the majority of cases their marriages failed. They often felt a distaste for sex, which put a great strain on marital relationships. Most repressed the memory of incest from childhood onwards. But the dark and shocking memories would not go away. They often returned in later life in the form of flashbacks, some of them triggered by intrusive surgery, illness or relationship problems. Coming to terms with an abused childhood in later life can be extremely painful and traumatic. But those who have spoken to us say that talking about the experience of abuse is an important first step in beginning to deal with these deep wounds from the past.

SYLVIA BAARDWYK

Sylvia was born in Tynemouth in 1910. Her father worked as a framebender on the docks but spent much of his time drinking and gambling. When she was only a few months old her parents separated. Unable to support Sylvia and her two brothers and sisters on her own their mother decided to emigrate to America in 1912 with the intention of sending for her children when she had found work. The children were split up and left in the care of various friends and relatives. Although she wrote, they never actually saw their mother again. Sylvia was taken in by a widowed friend of her mother's in South Shields, Mrs Foster. She was to live with her and her six seafaring sons in their small terraced house for the next fifteen years.

In 1926 Sylvia ran away to her aunt's and, after finding her sister, moved to London to work as manageress of a confectioner's. It was in London in 1930 that she met Peter, her husband. They married in 1933 and went on to have a son and a daughter. They lived very happily together until Peter's death in 1965. Sylvia had a brief second marriage in the 1970s but her husband died in 1979.

It is only in the last few years since Sylvia has lived alone that she has begun to relive some of her childhood memories. She has received no counselling although she has found it very therapeutic to write her memoirs and to talk to us about her experience of abuse.

"I would be about four years old when I was slept with her youngest son who would be thirteen, fourteen. This was because of lack of accommodation for separate sleeping for us all. It was then that he began to amuse himself and what I know now as masturbation to satisfy his urges.

I remember vividly how there was a window which I gazed through with the clouds, white clouds passing and a photograph of my sister and brother on that same wall. I could just lay there obeying his orders very bored, very tired and very relieved when it ceased. I was just being directed, 'Slower, quicker', and not quite responding as he wanted me to because I was tired.

I just had a feeling of acceptance, I'd always accepted, as a child, obedience to an older person. See all say nothing, touch nothing, don't tell tales or you'll be beaten.

He taught me different card games, taught me from being very young to play two-handed whist but his intentions were to get me alone. He'd indicate we go into the other room and I would just follow him. I didn't mind the game as long as we were playing cards but when we stopped playing I hated him, there was no escape. On one occasion I remember he began again his unwelcome attentions and on that occasion he said to me, 'Go and do a pee down in the yard.' And I found I was bleeding, not profusely, the skin would just be broken, he couldn't penetrate.

I began to have nightmares and I would wet the bed. And the next morning Mrs Foster would take that feather bed and put it on the floor and rub

Sylvia Baardwyk (*left*) and a school friend in 1918.

my nose in it and beat me. But I couldn't help it, I had cystitis very badly every night. I didn't know it was cystitis then but at any rate I had this inflammation. On one occasion I cried so hard she had to get out of the bed to me, used some lotion on me. Anything I complained about was not taken much notice of so I just bore it, endured it, it would go off in due course.

When he was about sixteen he became quite ill after an accident and laid up in bed for some months. I had to go to the library for him for books. And I used to read to him, the Boys' Papers, Sexton Blake and the like in that small bedroom with him, sitting by the window while he laid in bed and on this occasion he ordered me up onto his bed and played with me from the back passage with a pencil. All this was distressing.

I used to have terrific fits of depression and when I was left alone altogether in the house I remember sitting in the window looking out and I would cry and cry for a long time. Then I picked up a songbook, stood on a stool and sang, all the latest songs. My tears would dry. It was company to hear my voice, it wasn't so silent and I could imagine in a lot of ways that there was someone else there. I used to make my own kind of life, do a lot of pretending about having friends, wishful thinking.

As he got older he had begun to go out with ladies and this evening he had perfumed himself, dressed himself smartly, attractive and prepared himself with brilliantine, scent, talcum powder, that smell is still in my nostrils. He would put each cheek to me and ask was it a good scent. I would very quietly say, 'Yes'. I knew what would follow, practice before he kept his appointment. I was used as a guinea-pig for sexual advances. Loathsome, so loathsome, it was done standing up while he sat down and I just had to move backwards and forwards but the strange part about it is that I never looked, I never saw his

penis. No, no, I didn't like to even look at his face, his eyes, they were steely blue, like cruel. He was sadistic.

I just still thought that I wouldn't be believed if I spoke about it. He would be believed and I wouldn't and I began to wonder what sort of God was watching me all the time and then I began to resent the idea of God all the time. It wasn't logic any more and this grew gradually in my mind, that there was no God. I would still go to church but mainly to be able to get away from home.

I eventually confided in Mrs Foster's own daughter who had left home. She told her mother about it and Mrs Foster came up to me and said, 'What is this lie you are telling? Do you know that my home would be taken away from me and you would be put in a home?' I didn't reply, I didn't contradict, I knew it was useless. She said if any enquiries were made I was to tell them I was sitting on the park bench and I heard that story and I thought I would repeat it as if it happened to me. I knew she was protecting her son, she had silenced me. She just turned a blind eye to everything.

In desperation I did run away and found where my aunt was living. Of course he discovered where I'd gone and he appeared at my aunt's. His eyes blazed. He denied every word so my aunt took me to the police station, to a police doctor where I was examined in the lower areas. Very humiliating experience, especially with an authority such as the police doctor, a man. He seemed annoyed that he had been troubled, wasting his time. At the end of his examination we were directed to go to the police station next day and two policemen stood behind the counter, opened the book and said, 'No evidence'. I felt devastated. I felt that nobody was ever going to believe me.

This sexual abuse had its repercussions, all down the years, it was a handicap. I was fortunate in meeting a man who took me for what I was, without question about my background. I never spoke of my experiences until after the birth of my child which was sixteen years after my marriage. It was then that I could not always match up to my husband's virility and he began to think I was tiring of him. I thought it was right to tell him it was not him it was me, because of certain experiences when I was a child. He did not pursue what I had to say, he was more than ever considerate after I told him and never referred to it again.

Sylvia Baardwyk with her husband and daughter in the 1930s.
Sylvia married in 1933.

Only in the last few years I became ill and became an in-patient in a general hospital where I had extensive examinations, two up the back passage. That all triggered off memories of my childhood and on the last occasion when they attempted to put tubes down my throat I could not tolerate it any more and began to scream. All the memories flashed back into my mind. I felt I was being further abused and I ended up screaming out and asking for mercy. The nurses realized I was very distressed. All further tests were stopped. They would seem to stir a flashback of the whole of one's life and I began to talk and say how I'd been sexually abused while a child for the first time."

MAUD WOOD

Maud was born in Bradford in 1914. Her father was a dyer's labourer but it was her mother who supported the family, mainly through cleaning jobs and peddling door-to-door. Maud had four brothers and three sisters. When she was four and a half years old her father brought another woman to live with him. Maud's mother had no choice but to remain with her children in the family home although she didn't sleep with her husband from then onwards. Maud left school in 1928 and started work at fourteen as a spinner at the cotton mill.

When she was fifteen years old her father and his mistress were forced to leave the house after the women neighbours drew up a petition and threatened not to pay their rent if he was not evicted. They had got tired of his constant drunkenness and womanizing although Maud does not know whether or not they suspected him of abusing her. Maud met her husband in 1932 and thinking that she needed her father's permission to marry she went to see him for the first time since he had left the house. She never saw him again and married the next year when she was nineteen.

Her husband worked as a fruiterer's labourer but was unemployed for six years before going away to fight in the army in the Second World War. Maud had a son and a daughter. Although Maud has been able to speak to her family about most aspects of her abuse

Maud Wood aged eighteen.

To my Darling
with all my
Enduring
Love
xxx

experience she has had severe problems with her nerves and depression from time to time during her life. For many years she felt very guilty about what had happened in her childhood and still has nightmares about the abuse.

"He always wanted his own way, me father. He had first pick of any food we had on the table but he never brought the money in for it. Me mother had to work to look after us and he wouldn't lift a finger to help her. All he was interested in was his women.

When I was four and a half years of age he brought a fancy woman into the house. Me mother was confined in bed so he brought this woman in to sort of look after me but me mother's bed being by the sitting-room wall, she could hear this woman creeping up to bed with me father. He'd done this before to my mother, so she knew what were going on.

When I was about ten years of age school gymslips were coming into fashion and I was talking to me younger sister about how much I wanted one of these gymslips. Me father piped up, he says, 'I'll buy you the gymslip, I'll give you a shilling a week.' So I thought, 'Oh good', because up to that point he'd never done anything really wrong to me.

Now then, after I got the first shilling I'm in bed and he creeps up and gets onto the bed. I thought to myself, 'What's this?' And he starts manoeuvring about with me nightgown and then I didn't know what it were, his organ. He got on top of me and he put it sort of into me and I didn't say anything. He went downstairs sort of holding hisself.

I thought that was what I were gettin' for the shilling, that's what I had to do. I got the shilling at the morning to go a school with, to take for the gymslip, but you see after that were paid for he still went on and I didn't get no more shillings.

When I got home from school me mother used to be charring so there were just him in the house. I used to go out in the streets, I could throw it off when I went out to play, I never thought of it. It was an escape. I used to make up scenes from the silent films with the other children. They always had an 'appy ending and they always had me for the heroine, Pearl White. I were fastened up on lamppost then one of the boys'd come and rescue me. When I got rescued with the hero I was wishing to God somebody would really come and rescue me.

But then me father'd start calling me in to wash up about eight o'clock. When I 'eard, oh I can 'ear 'im in the distance now, I can 'ear him shouting,

Maud Wood's father and mother pictured in the late 1930s.

'Maudie, come in and wash up'. I can 'ear it. I can 'ear it in me distant mind I can 'ear it. There was no delaying it and I knew I had to go in to him.

I'd have to wash up then get up to bed but I never went to sleep, 'cos the frightening part about it was when he used to creep up the steps and open the bedroom door. Y'see, there were a gas lamp so it cast a bit of a shadow over it. I'd see him coming over, my heart used to race then and I thought, 'Hey up, this is it'. I went to sleep when I knew that was over, that were done with for that night. That's how I lived through it.

Now there were other times it happened. When you've been asleep at night, I mean, you got up next morning, you went to school, well you forgot about it. It were the days when it 'appened at the dinner-time that upset me mostly. I had to come 'ome from school for me meals and everyone else would be out so he knew, he knew he were safe then, as safe as 'ouses. I knew when I get into 'ouse what I got, I thought meself, 'Well, when I get 'ome he'll be waiting for me with this sort of a dinner on the table, bit of sausage or sommat like that.' And then I'd be down on the floor. I got really sickened, he used to go to the sink when he'd done the manoeuvring about with me and run his, his, what I know now as his penis, under the tap. Them days I couldn't bring meself to do nowt really.

My mother worked that hard, I just couldn't bring myself to tell her. She got home late from charring and I'd be upstairs in bed, she was just worn out from all the work to keep us fed and clothed. And anyway, you never mentioned sex in those days, I wouldn't have known how to tell her. They didn't even read psalms at school when there were 'breasts' or 'pregnant' in them, it was really very hard.

Now that went on until I were about eleven. Then I'd lumps in me groins and they were 'urting. So I thought I'd better say, get it all off me chest. 'Cos I knew it must have been the weight of 'im on me. I told me mother then, I 'ad to and I had to go to the doctor's. He said to me mother, 'Well,' he said, 'you can take him to court but I'm afraid you'll not get very far, 'cos children are always liars.' So me mother had to put up with it but she give me father it, she nearly killed him. And she made sure that I never went to bed on me own no more. I slept with her when me mother come in.

The happiest day of my life is when I come home from the mill and he'd gone. Me mother says, 'He's been thrown out.' The neighbours signed a petition saying they would withhold the rent if me father weren't thrown out. Well, the woman next door lived wall-to-wall and they could hear it carry on, they could 'ear it and they thought my mother'd had enough. So she got the petition up and he had to go, take his fancy woman with 'im.

But even then, after that ceased the sexual come stirring in me and I tried sort of abusing meself. I didn't know it were abusing, God forbid I didn't, but I used to do it, the same motion on the bed as he did to me.

When I got to thirteen years of age I said to myself that I wasn't gonna do this thing any more. Being a Roman Catholic I had to go to confession and I had to tell the priest that I done an immodest action. It were forbidden, 'owt like that, to touch yerself even. Never asked you what you'd done, 'Take for your penance three Hail Marys or three Our Fathers', he'd say and then he'd free me from me sin, you know like, give you absolution.

But eventually I had to tell meself, 'No more, never again, never.' And I never did, I never touched myself from that day forth. It breaks me 'eart when I think about it, and I told my husband about it and all me family knows about it, but they didn't know about what I did to meself 'cos that I kept a secret. I carried that sin for up to me fifties, I still thought it were my sin.

I've had one or two nervous breakdowns, tell you the truth, I've been in a psychiatric hospital. The effect of the breakdowns was like living in a grey twilight, no matter how the sun shines you're still grey. And I still have nightmares. It haunts me, it never leaves me."

DAVID BARRON

David was found abandoned on a doorstep when he was only a few months old in 1925 and taken to Street Lane Orphanage in Leeds where he stayed until he was five. He was then fostered out to a woman who lived in Armley, Leeds. For the next nine years, in her care, David was neglected, starved and physically abused. He was made to sleep on the floor in an attic room and was forced to beg for scraps of food from door-to-door. Although he was sent to a special school he never received a proper education.

In 1939 a neighbour reported David's foster mother to the authorities. Her home and David's situation were inspected and she was taken to court charged with cruelty. After the case David was told he was being taken away from his foster mother and sent to a home. In actual fact he was taken to the Mid-Yorkshire Mental Institution at Wixley near York where he was to be locked away for the next twenty-five years. He was only released when the National Council for Civil Liberties took up his case in 1964 and he received a full discharge.

David was given little or no support after leaving Wixley and found it difficult to find work and accommodation. He had various jobs around the North-West but was often discriminated against because of his past. In the early 1970s he was working as a hotel porter in Blackpool when he met his future wife. Together they moved to Manchester and married in 1974. However, the marriage was annulled after eighteen months and soon after that David suffered a severe breakdown. He was sent to Armley Jail in Leeds after taking an overdose but in the hospital wing of the prison he smashed a window and ate the glass in another suicide bid. David spent the next ten months in Pinderford Hospital in Wakefield and attempted suicide on numerous occasions. Eventually he confided in his doctor the reason for his depression, the traumatic memories of Wixley and the fear that he himself would become an abuser. He was prescribed hormone treatment, a drug called stilbistrol.

Since then, David has found his own flat in Manchester where he has many friends and has written his autobiography, A Price to Be Born. *He now gives lectures at schools and colleges in the North-West talking about his life.*

"They said, 'David, you're going to a nice big home where you'll get plenty of food and you'll have everything you can think of, pictures, concerts, you name it.' He made me believe the moon was made of green cheese and at that point I was taken away and I was taken to Wixley.

Going up this big drive and I could see this clock and all the people working in the allotments on each side. I was so excited I kept saying, 'Will we be having cinema shows?' 'Oh yes, we're having those,' they said, 'Oh, we wish you all the very best and we do hope you'll be very, very happy here.'

And then I was taken down to Ward One, that ward put fear into me from the day I went into it. This attendant took me down and he had this big massive chain, locked the door behind me. I could see grown-ups, all sat in various places, the first thing I noticed was the windows were barred. This attendant took me to a little cell room and said, 'Right, this'll be your room, take your clothes off, fold them up.' 'Now,' he said, 'David you will do this and if you don't you'll get a damn good beating.' He pushed me in and then he slammed the door. And that door sounded very heavy to me.

It was open dormitories, beds all the way down the side. After half-past six all the lights was out but unfortunately that's when patients used to find that you had company. You knew damn well what was taking place, it was either your bed which was going to be visited or they were visiting other patients' beds to commit these acts. I knew exactly what was going to take place but there was some poor souls who just didn't know what time of day it was, they were easy meat.

It wasn't just with patients, it was with staff alike. It wasn't an uncommon thing to find an attendant in bed with a patient. They'd do all the other things which you should never have done. They did things which I didn't understand, they'd ask you to roll over on your side and they would insert their penis in your body, or get you to roll over. In fact on one occasion I had blood drawn. They were like raving wild animals, it all happened so quick you couldn't... I mean it, they had that upper hand. It was always done so sort of violent.

Why didn't I go and complain to the authorities? You could not complain to the authority, they were the authority. They didn't have a fear of what they'd done, they didn't have a fear about me going and telling anybody. And I was terrified for the simple reason that I'd no one to go to. If I tried to tell someone, well then they'd just simply get you in your room, two or three of them, and you'd get a severe beating.

Or they could always use threats against you. They'd say, 'Oh, you've not done this right, you haven't done that right, so therefore if I report this to the superintendent you'll be down to Ward One.' That was a notorious ward, for punishment, which to this very day I have nightmares about. So if an attendant wanted to commit these acts of sex with you, you either let him do it or you risked the fear of God. You literally went through hell. They would make things up and you could be dumped in Ward One and as far as you was concerned the key would be thrown away.

I did rebel from one attendant, I lashed out at him when he tried to get into my bed. But what he did, next day, he got a towel and stuck it in a cold bath, wrapped it round me and he was beating me. That way there'd be no bruising.

It's yer entire body in pain. I went through hell and it was affecting my mind. But it was like between the devil and the deep blue seas, you had nobody to turn to and it all was starting to roll into me mind... First and foremost why should I have been put into that mental hospital in the first place? Why should I have to undergo all this?

So as I got older I realized that what was going on, it wasn't a right thing. So when these so-called people used to come to me with their threats I just simply used to say to them, 'Right, go ahead, go and report me to the superintendent I couldn't care less. If I've got to go to Ward One I'll go.'

When I began to grow up, I was then getting urges but the urges were wrong, weren't the natural urges at all. I just didn't understand it. It was only when I left the institution that I really, really knew. I could literally have gone doing what had been done to me.

When I was out I was just left to fend for meself really. But I had two stigmas to deal with. Not only had I come out after being in a mental hospital for twenty-five years but also it was that thought all the time of the sexual abuse that I had suffered. I would get these urges and sweat would pour out of me. Now, was I gonna go round and commit the offences against young boys as what those dirty beasts had done to me, it was a cry in the night. I thought, 'No way.' But the only way I could think to get out of this hell was to do with meself, to finish meself off.

I just took an overdose and the second time I attempted suicide I was placed in Armley Jail Hospital Wing, I was put into a straitjacket. I tried to explain to them but they just didn't want to know. I put my bare fist through a window and smashed the entire glass to fragments and I tried to swallow the whole lot, swallow it down with bread. I thought that would finally see me off.

Finally a doctor did listen to me and he said they had a drug, an experiment which would take all the urges away and I was one of the very first to take this drug which alters your hormones. I went through eternal hell with it, the pain, agony day in and day out but I didn't mind and from that day to this I've never looked back, but what a price I've paid. I can hold me head up to the grown-ups.

Naturally then, I wanted to try to do what other grown-ups do in the outside world, get married. But there was more to it that I didn't understand. There was love and the beds and everything that went with that. I can remember that first night, the honeymoon, I screamed when she wanted to indulge in the proper thing and I just darted out of the bedroom. It wasn't her fault but in my mind I just had those beasts tampering with my body and I pleaded with her not to touch me. The marriage had to be annulled.

When I'm lonely I feel very depressed sometimes and of course the institution comes back all the time. But there's sometimes when I've thought I wanted to go back, when I feel there's no place out in society for me. Then my mind goes back just like a tape running back, it goes back in time. And then I just put a record on, put a few tunes on, I love music, and try to get it out of my system."

CAROLE MANDEVILLE

Carole was born in 1943 in West Farleigh, near Maidstone, and grew up there with her two brothers and one sister. Her father was a lecturer in business studies at the local Further Education College. Carole left school when she was seventeen to work as a shorthand typist. In 1963 she gave up her job and began a correspondence course to get enough 'O' and 'A' levels to go to university. She did a

BA degree in English and Politics at Newcastle University. After graduating when she was twenty-six Carole became a trainee psychiatric social worker and then worked for the British Council in London and Birmingham. She married in 1972 and had two children.

Carole became assistant to the Director of the Samaritans in Canterbury and then a councillor for schools. In 1987 she was diagnosed as having multiple sclerosis. A year later she started having flashback memories of her childhood experiences of abuse. Over the next two years as her memory came back the MS symptoms disappeared. She is now left with only a few occasional signs of the illness. Carole still works as a school counsellor as well as having her own private practice where she specializes in working with adults and children who have been abused. She has recently finished writing an autobiographical account of her experiences, Not Enough Angels*.*

"I had had MS for about a year and a half when I first started to remember. I was round at a friend's house one evening and she had a huge painting of her father in the kitchen. She talked a lot about him and I began to realize more than I had before that I couldn't actually remember very much about my own father. In fact the only things that I really remembered about my childhood were where I lived, and where I went to school and the fact that I'd been hit and that's all I remembered really.

I suppose she spent most of the evening talking about her father and I had nothing to say, I had no memory at all, somehow I'd lost all my childhood memory. It was that night that I began to get flashbacks.

I was lying in bed and the feeling came over me that I was suffocating. I felt as if I wanted to be sick, I felt as if I had something in my throat, that my windpipe was blocked, my head threw back in a sort of convulsion and my body went into a convulsion and I felt like a rag doll.

I suppose it must have been a couple of weeks later when I had a specific flashback of being sexually abused. It was then, actually smelling my father's pyjamas and feeling his body on top of me that I realized that I'd been sexually abused from babyhood until puberty, not just by my father but by some of his relations, including my grandmother.

It was very hard remembering all that. I felt the feelings for the first time, I felt the physical pain for the first time. As a child I had put in place good defence mechanisms forgetting some of the stuff almost as soon as it happened and, of course, as an adult I'd forgotten the whole thing. I'd be talking to people and another flashback would happen. Somehow I had to find the will just to go on acting as if nothing had happened. It was like a continuous nightmare. The memories were flooding in nightmares and flashbacks. I felt as if I was being raped and beaten every day and that's virtually how it was because everything came in a flood so that over two years I relived an extent of eleven years of sexual abuse.

On the face of it we were a respectable middle-class family. How little people know what goes on behind those respectable middle-class doors, terror, really. My father was a teacher and he taught in a local college, he had a good job, he was a self-made man. And yet, the other side of him was the reign of terror he exerted in our house, the beatings that we got, the abuse, the fact that he did whatever he wanted to do, that he was a psychopath and that he had no conscience.

On holiday he got into his very boyish mood, he liked being the master of ceremonies. When we went to the seaside he would turn into his boyish self and play games on the sands but the feeling was that we couldn't succeed in whatever he wanted us to do. We were always lacking so that we didn't get the games right, we didn't score enough runs, and then he would swim off. He was a very thick-set man, very muscular, and he would always swim right out to sea until he disappeared. My mother and I would be sitting there on the sand waiting for him to come back, it was as if he was defying life, he had a death wish. He was trying to evoke emotion in all of us so we sat in a state of terror waiting for him to come back. Then he would come back sort of triumphant. I was terrified of him, I mean the fear that I felt around him was tremendous, I felt absolute fear of him and he ruled the house like a tyrant.

My first memory of sexual abuse by my father is when I was about four or five and he abused me in the bath by inserting things into me and making me perform oral sex and anal sex. I was bathed by him entirely on my own and when I remembered that it felt to me as if my mother had chosen me to be the one who would in a sense take care of my father's sexual perversions.

I lived a life in hiding really. I hid as much from him as I could and I had very little contact with my mother at all. At an emotional level I was pretty well numb. I had no sense of family, we lived in isolation. There were six people in that house and yet everyone was isolated from the other. So I was very lonely as a child, I found it very difficult to relate to other children. I spent a lot of the time out of the house wandering the countryside to be away from it. I played in the streams and the woods for hours on end looking at the sky and the trees. Countryside to me still partially means a very deep loneliness.

Carole Mandeville with one of her brothers on a family holiday
in the late 1940s.

When I was eight my father began taking me to my aunt's house in Hampshire and at the time I felt chosen and I felt special and I felt loved for the first time in my life. Half-way there we stopped at a huge hotel. I'd never been taken out to lunch before. My father treated me with such kindness and generosity, I'd never experienced that before in him. I remember so clearly that the dining-room consisted just of couples, no children, and he asked me what I wanted to eat. I looked at the cheaper things and he could see me looking at them, he said, 'No, no, choose something expensive, whatever you want'. So I went for this amazing ice-cream which was white and pink with a sort of frilled wafer on the top. I had that feeling of elation and I remember looking around the dining-room full of the other couples and I felt like a couple. I know the thought went through my mind that I was his wife.

We then went on to my aunt's house and the feeling of specialness continued. They sat playing cards and they were drinking sherry. My father offered me sherry and anything he offered was impossible to refuse, but at the same time I did want to accept it because I had this feeling of grown-upness. I don't know how much I drank but it felt like quite a lot and looking back, you know, I know that the whole thing was a conspiracy so that he could rape me, which is what he did later that night when I'd gone to bed.

He came to the door of my room and stood at the door and the light was behind him. I was pleased to see him because he was smiling, and I thought to myself, 'I am so much wanted and loved, he loves me now and he's coming to say goodnight.' But he said, in a very strange sing-songy voice, 'I've come to say goodnight to you my darling.' I know that my child sense began to feel that there was something strange about it, but the other feeling of being loved and wanted overrode that. He knelt down by my bed and kissed me with his tongue in my mouth, and then he raped me.

In the morning when we were leaving he said to me in the car, 'Last night,' he said, 'that was just a bit of fun.' He didn't need to tell me that I should not tell anyone.

He took me away to my aunt's three or four times. And going home for me was always filled with terror and twice I tried to kill myself. It was like being an animal trapped with no way of relieving the pain that I'd just experienced. Of course he drove like a maniac and as we got nearer to home I tried to open the car door and jump out and he leant across and grabbed the car door and then he hit me with the back of his hand across my face and said, 'D'you want to kill us both you stupid little bitch.'

Carole Mandeville's father and mother outside their home in 1948.

I was failing at school, very depressed, very suicidal. But I couldn't tell anybody what was happening to me, it never really occurred to me because I had no feeling. I think because the fear around my father was so huge. He even threatened me with being put into a mental institution. He would call me crazy and drive me past the local mental hospital, I was about ten or so, and said that he would have me put away.

He stopped abusing me when I reached puberty. I remember he and my aunt and uncle (his sister and brother-in-law) were in our house for Christmas and I'd started having periods. At first I thought to myself, 'He's done something to me again.' But I couldn't figure it out because I couldn't put a recent incident to it. My mother hadn't told me anything about periods but she led me through to the bathroom and gave me a very brief explanation. We had to go through the kitchen where my father and my uncle and my aunt were there, and one of them said, laughing, 'Well, that's the end of your little bit of fun Tommy.' Then they all burst out laughing. My mother pushed me through the door so that I wouldn't hear it, wouldn't hear their laughter, but it rang in my ears and I felt, I felt dirty.

All these memories came back to me when I was trying to cope with being ill with MS and my marriage was breaking up because of it. I found it difficult to relate to other people. I had a feeling of not being real, a feeling of hollowness, a feeling of not belonging in this world as if I was adrift somewhere about a mile above it. It certainly affected my marriage, my sense of connection with my husband and my relationship with my children.

I wished for two years that I'd never remembered. I felt terrorized by remembering and I wished that I hadn't. It was the rage inside me which drove me physically. But now my MS has gone. It was the abuse locked inside my body that produced itself in an outward form as MS, and as I worked through the memories my body recovered.

Survivors of child abuse don't suffer it the once, sometimes they don't feel it initially, but at some level they do and it goes into their bodies and is stored there as a memory, and when the memory comes back they suffer it over and over and over and over again."

6

STREET LIVES
HOMELESSNESS

Every year in the 1920s and 1930s many thousands of young Irish men and women disembarked at Liverpool docks dreaming of a new life in England. At the very least they expected adventure and the chance to earn a lot more than they could at home. Blessed by the local priest, pockets full of 'luck money' and with a black bag containing a change of clothes slung over their shoulders, these hopeful travellers from County Mayo and County Clare formed part of an age-old mass migration across the Irish Sea. They wanted to escape from the poverty and the grim subsistence economy which overshadowed life in the new Republic of Ireland. Many made it, eventually. But on the way they might find themselves homeless and friendless, facing even greater hardships than they had in Ireland. It was no accident that most commentators on the low life of the doss-houses of inter-war England and Scotland detected a strong Irish presence. Just several weeks after leaving their mothers for the first time – and through no fault of their own – many young hopefuls found themselves sleeping in ditches, hedges, haystacks and squalid lodging houses. This Irish sub-culture formed the most visible section of the homeless population of Britain in the first half of this century.

Most vulnerable to homelessness were the seasonal migratory workers. They harvested the potato and sugar beet crops in Scotland, Yorkshire and the East of England. There was a demand for casual labour in most rural areas at harvest time but employment might be only for a few days or weeks and the freelance agricultural labourers had to make their way from one farm to another in their quest for work. Sometimes this might involve walking long distances from one part of Britain to another. Word of mouth was very important in passing on knowledge of where work was to be found. The men on the tramp often slept rough and even when they were working for farmers

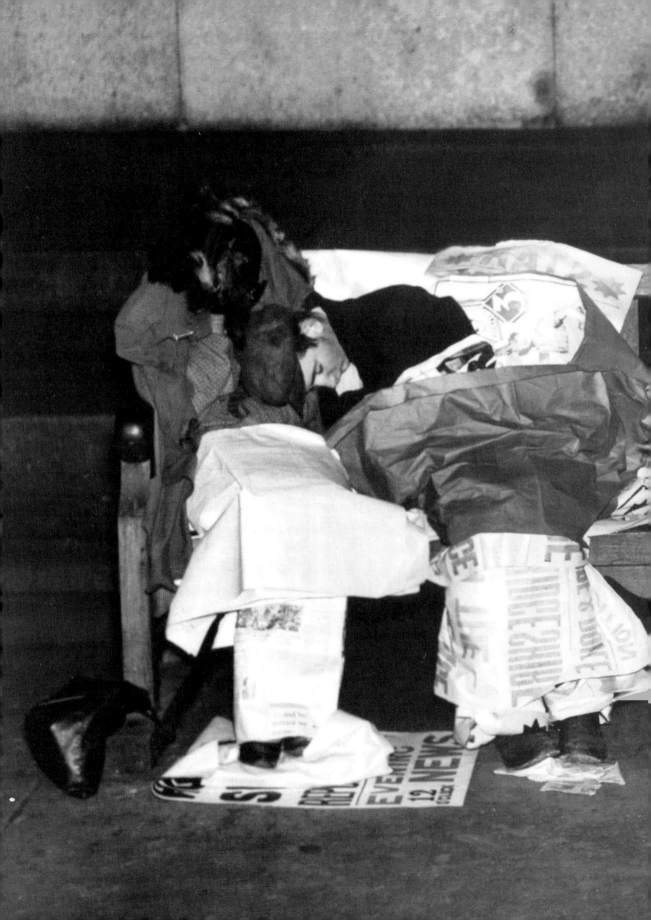

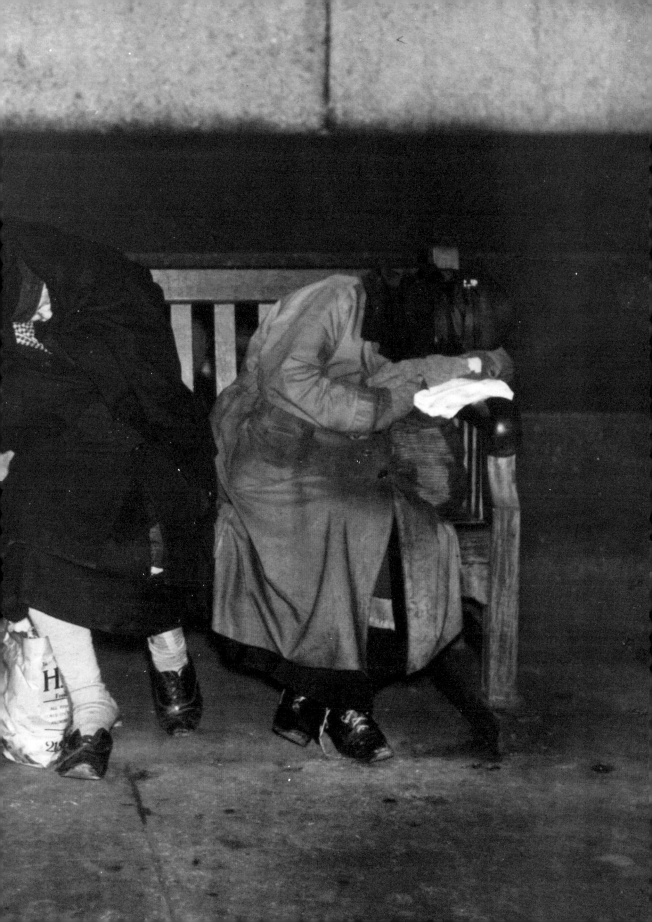

the accommodation was not much better. Most were offered a bed of straw in old farm buildings and barns which had no facilities at all. A similar pattern of work and tramping between jobs operated in the building industry, the other big employer of casual Irish labour. Navvies would walk the length and breadth of the country from one building-site to another. The willingness to sleep and live rough was seen by foremen as the hallmark of a good worker. Those who arrived for work too smartly dressed would often be rejected as 'kid glove navvies' or 'passengers'.

The young men who suddenly gravitated into this harsh life on the margins of society frequently owed their survival to the help and advice given by older navvies with years of experience of life on the road. Although their culture was hard and sometimes violent – with an elaborate pecking order based on physical strength – they could also be generous and protective to those new to the game. Advice would be given on what to wear to best withstand the elements (long reefer jackets and heavy working boots were the standard uniform), how to 'drum up' mugs of tea by the roadside, how to beg, the best places to sleep and where to get work.

The Irish navvies and migrants formed part of a shifting, homeless population officially estimated at around 40–80 000 during the first decades of the century. Numbers went up during times of recession, for example in the early 1930s when unemployment was at its peak, as the search for work and eviction forced more onto the road. Official surveys of homelessness before the last war however were very limited and incomplete, seriously underestimating the numbers who had no roof over their heads. The London County Council – one of the most vigilant of the local authorities in dealing with this problem – only covered selected spots in the heart of London like the railway termini, the Embankment and Leicester Square in its head count of those sleeping rough in the capital. Both national and local governments were most concerned with re-housing the two million or so people who were living in slum conditions and in homes classified as unfit for human habitation. The 'vagrant problem' received far less attention and remained largely hidden. George Orwell's *Down and Out in Paris and London*, published in 1933, was one of the few attempts to expose the plight of the homeless at the time.

Previous page: Men and women sleeping rough in London in 1930.
The homeless population rose during the depression of the 1930s, when unemployment was at its peak.

A drunk being arrested in Dundee in 1910. Alcohol was the traditional
escape for many homeless people.

The hard-core members of this army of the poor and dispossessed were –
unlike the Irish navvies and migrants – permanent 'vagrants' and remained in
the same area for long periods. There were disabled veterans of the Great War
who could no longer find work. There were alcoholics: excessive drinking was
the traditional escape from poverty, ill health and failed marriages. And there
were 'professional' tramps who made a living from begging and petty crime.
Most of the homeless were male and single. Early surveys showed a ratio of
around ten males to every one female without a fixed address.

In 1926 social reformer Mrs Cecil Chesterton left her comfortable middle-
class home to find out what life was like on the streets for women. She

A Glasgow family being evicted
in the 1930s. Rent increases
and absolute poverty forced
many families onto the streets.

A London Soup Kitchen in the 1920s. A free meal provided a welcome relief for those accustomed to the hardships of living on the streets.

discovered that a substantial number of these homeless women made what little money they could from prostitution. They had generally been driven onto the streets by economic misfortune. 'Generally speaking it's poverty, and very largely, the shortage of housing, illness, bad luck, and increase of rent, which drive many a decent woman out of her home and force her to become a tramp on the road, or to sell matches in the street.' (From the book *In Darkest London* by Mrs Cecil Chesterton, published in 1928.)

The homeless spent some of the time sleeping rough and some of the time – especially the cold winter months – sleeping in various houses and institutions provided for them. Most towns and cities had common lodging houses, the age old place of shelter for the impoverished, for thieves and for prostitutes. London boasted 450 registered lodging houses in the 1900s. These 'dens of infamy' had been cleaned up and controlled by local authorities in the Victorian period, becoming regimented and barrack-like places. But at least they provided some shelter. In addition there were still many unregistered 'doss-houses' in the inter-war years. In the thirties Orwell reported that at the bottom of the lodging house market there were still 'Twopenny Hangovers' where you spent the night sitting on a bench leaning over a rope which was unceremoniously dropped in the morning by an assistant. If you only had four (old) pence you had to make do with a night in a bug-ridden coffin bed with tarpaulin covers. The set meals in these places were little more than bread and dripping or bread and cheese.

Then there was the casual ward of the workhouse, known to tramps as 'the spike'. Here accommodation could often be equally bleak and barbaric, especially in rural areas where little money was invested in Poor Law institutions. The spike's guests would normally be expected to 'pay' for their night's accommodation the next day by cleaning, doing odd jobs, chopping up firewood or breaking stones.

By the inter-war years the main provider of shelter for the homeless was the Salvation Army. It appeared on the hostel scene in the late 1880s, prompted by the horror felt by its founder William Booth at the large number of destitutes sleeping out in London at the time. By the 1930s it was providing more than 4000 beds in London alone in a network of hostels with evocative names like 'The Ark', 'The Harbour' and 'The Lighthouse'. The accommodation offered by the 'Sally Ann' was cheap and clean, and for a few pence the residents could enjoy a substantial meal including soup nicknamed 'Allelujah Stew'. But the attempt to save the souls of the inmates with endless bible-punching sermons, prayers and hymn singing was – according to Orwell and others – immensely unpopular with the world-weary clientele.

Children were the most invisible of all the homeless groups in the first decades of the century. On the night of 13 February 1914, only five children were discovered sleeping rough in London. After this the London County Council censuses recorded no further cases of homeless children. In the 1920s the official estimate of the numbers of children in the casual wards of the

nation's workhouses was around fifty on any one night. By the 1930s, according to official surveys and statistics, there were virtually no homeless children. These figures are, however, grossly misleading. The great Victorian scandal of hordes of waifs and strays adrift in the new industrial towns and cities had admittedly been largely solved by compulsory state schooling, legislation against child labour and more rigorous controls on child vagrancy. Those who slipped through the net – orphans, truants, disabled children, delinquents, and so on – ended up as inmates in a network of punitive 'live in' institutions. Overall, at the start of the century more than 100 000 children were in orphanages, children's homes, reformatories, industrial schools and other similar institutions. What the official statistics missed, though, were the substantial numbers of children who absconded from them. They were on the run, hiding from the authorities – and homeless. The testimony of these runaways vividly illustrates how they survived and avoided detection by the police, by school attendance officers and by early social workers. Some were taken under the wing of tramps, prostitutes and criminals. The deal frequently involved some involvement in petty crime. And groups thought to be beyond the pale of respectable society, like street-market traders, travelling fairs or rag-and-bone men, would often feed and protect these ragged children in exchange for their labour.

These boys and girls who – for a time at least – vanished from the official records were joined by others escaping from family life. Extreme poverty, drunkenness and harsh authoritarian attitudes towards children drove unknown numbers of children to run away from home. So too did cruel step-parents. Added to this some children – most of them from poor working-class backgrounds – ran away for a few days or even weeks, sleeping rough, for an adventure. In sea-ports like Bristol and Newcastle poor children regularly tried to stow away, some of them imagining that they would enjoy a more comfortable and privileged life style once they arrived elsewhere in the Empire. Interviews reveal that some older children were actually deliberately made homeless for a time by their parents – they might be locked out while their parents went away for holidays. The 'home alone' problem is certainly nothing new. Much of this homelessness seems to have gone unrecorded by the police

Previous page: **Farthing breakfasts at the Salvation Army around 1900. Although there were few cases of homeless children officially recorded at this time, in fact, many children were living on the streets.**

Dr Barnardo's orphans in the 1900s when more than 100 000 were in similar institutions. Their harsh regimes forced many children to run away and attempt to survive on the streets.

or by social workers. Child protection agencies were certainly less vigilant and more relaxed about the notion of homeless children than they are today.

The Second World War massively increased the homeless population in Britain. It changed its character too. Suddenly, respectable families whose homes had been bombed found themselves without a roof over their heads and with nowhere to go. During the first month of the blitz, which began in the autumn of 1940, around a quarter of a million people were made homeless in London alone.

There was a desperate shortage of accommodation and help for homeless families. Voluntary groups like the WVS, the YMCA and the Salvation Army struggled to provide clothing and food for this new army of destitutes. Most were directed to rest centres run by the local authorities but these quickly became swamped in the worst hit cities. Official plans to evacuate the homeless were often delayed and disrupted. Many went to stay with relatives,

A homeless woman in London in 1938. Early surveys showed a ratio of ten men to every woman without a fixed address.

often resulting in serious overcrowding. But countless thousands were forced to set up makeshift homes, with what personal possessions they could salvage – in sheds, Anderson shelters, cars and lorries, warehouses, church crypts, under railway arches and on London underground stations.

The wartime homeless problem was made worse by the nightly exodus from the blitzed cities into the safety of the countryside. Most slept rough in fields, under hedges or in barns. Disused coal-pit workings were popular as they seemed to offer protection from the elements and from stray bombs. Some families even began living in caves. Fleeing Londoners discovered a series of caverns at Chislehurst in Kent. After a week of the Blitz more than 8000 Londoners were living there. To begin with they slept on the stone floor but after several weeks beds, armchairs and tables were transported down in carts and lorries. Similar patterns of cave-dwelling developed close to several other badly hit cities. In Bristol the Portway caves in the Avon Gorge were quickly colonized by terrified and homeless families.

The Blitz on most British cities ended in summer 1941 and most families returned home. The emergency services – now under less pressure – were better able to provide for those whose homes had been destroyed. But there was a new problem. Housing repairs on bomb-damaged houses were invariably slow and piecemeal, and around a quarter of a million families were forced to live in primitive conditions with blown-out windows, missing doors, badly leaking roofs and an irregular gas and water supply. The war left the nation with a massive housing shortage: most official estimates admitted a shortage of at least a million dwellings. In 1945 the demobilized troops came home to a housing crisis – great swathes of the towns and cities they had left had turned to rubble. It was all very different to the vision of a family home for all that had been promoted by wartime propaganda.

Some were so desperate for a home that they turned to squatting. First to be occupied were disused army camps. The squatting movement began spontaneously in Scunthorpe in the summer of 1946 when some homeless families who had been sleeping in the back row of the local cinema came across a deserted gun site with Nissen huts on the outskirts of the town. They moved in, soon others joined them and within three months it was reported in the House of Commons that almost 50 000 people were in occupation of more than 1000 such camps all over Britain. In September the Communist Party stepped up the agitation by organizing squats for the homeless in a number of blocks of luxury flats in the West End including the Duchess of Bedford flats in Kensington. The London squats were short-lived and the Communist Party activists arrested. But the new Labour government – committed to providing homes for all – was more sympathetic to the army camp squatters and local authorities were instructed to reconnect essential services to the camps. Some of the squats lingered on for several years.

The fifties were to see a lower rate of homelessness than at any time before or since in recent British history. A sustained housing drive by post-war governments – Labour, for example, built more than a million high-quality council homes between 1945 and 1951 – massively increased the nation's housing stock. The development of the Welfare State, with more provision for those in most need, reduced the numbers forced onto the streets. And with full employment and greater affluence the tramping workseeker increasingly became a figure of the past. The National Assistance Board took over and improved the old casual wards, which now became known as 'reception centres'. The numbers using them, however, reduced dramatically and as a result many were closed down. The 134 centres in 1948 were reduced to just 43 by 1960. In the fifties the London County Council found that so few people were sleeping rough that they decided to discontinue their regular surveys.

One kind of homelessness though was on the increase in the fifties. More and more young teenage girls were running away from home. Behind this much publicized problem lay the demand of young people for more independence and freedom from parental control. Our interviews also suggest that in a number of cases sexual abuse by fathers or brothers was involved. At this time many teenage runaways made for Blackpool with its glamorous holiday image and the hope of casual work on the sea-front without too many questions being asked. But some of these homeless girls had to turn to prostitution as the only way to survive. In this they were following in the footsteps of all the earlier generations of women who had been reduced to a life on the street.

JOHN NEARY

John, born in County Mayo in the west of Ireland in 1909, was the oldest of five brothers. His father was a farm manager. Unable to find permanent work in Ireland, John left for England when he was sixteen. He worked for a few months on a sugar beet farm in Yorkshire. For the next year John was on the road, working when he could on farms or building-sites. He was homeless during that time, sleeping in ditches, old farm buildings, 'kip houses' or Salvation Army hostels. In 1937 he married and found a job working for Ford's. He and his wife, Vera, were given a council house in Dagenham. They have three children and all live together in the same home. John has recently written his autobiography.

"The first thing you did was borrow the cost to get to the promised land and that was what we done. Me dear old mam took me to the station. I'd never even been on a train before. Your sole worldly goods was wrapped in a

John Neary (*left*) with his mother and younger brother shortly before he left Ireland to look for work in England in 1925.

black cloth, a bundle, and while we was on the platform that morning the older people 'ud come with their luck money, they give you a shilling for luck. The women was crying out, 'Write when you land.' The local priest came on to the platform to give you his blessing, to wish you well, shook hands and gave you his blessing. The local shopkeepers come because their trade depended on what money we sent home. Many of the local townspeople sent teams of step dancers on to the station to cheer you up but there was a lot of crying, very, very emotional. The last thing my mother done was give me an old two and sixpenny piece ... her parting gift for luck, and I needed a lot. It was like taking the lambs to slaughter, some were going to far off America, some going to Britain, some going to Australia. They was putting the life's blood of our nation on board the immigrant ship, and that's the way it was.

But I was going to send money, I was going to be rich, going to Britain. I'd never been away from home, never seen the seaside before. But you didn't realize how bad it was till the end of the day when you'd been about ten or twelve hours travelling and you missed yer mother's cooking. You thought there was something nice at the end of the rainbow but you had a shock.

I got to Yorkshire where I was meant to be working for these farmers. They hired me and some other boys to work in the sugar beet fields or maybe the potato fields. They took us in an open back car away out to the farm, gave us a bed, a bundle of straw each and a horse. No cooking facilities, no toilets, no washing. The work was terrible because you was mud up to your eyes. You crept along the ground for quickness, you couldn't keep your back bent so you went on knees and sacks. The hours was terrible, long, long hours. Out at dawn in the morning 'til late at night, piece rate. And after just a few weeks they told us there was no more work, the contract was finished.

We had to find work but there wasn't any so we started to walk. We walked to Leeds, eighteen miles. It took us nearly two days and I went to a building-site for work and this bloke said, 'No, you're not one of us. You're in the wrong street mate. How the hell do you go into a trench with them bloody shoes you got on?' If I'd put mud on me boots then I'd have got a job. The old navvies they always had their slouch and their trench and their duffel coat, the heavy boots, they got a job straight away. Me, nobody would employ me, 'You're too young, you've no experience.'

Somebody told us about the spike where you could stay for a night but when we got to this workhouse, big building, they wouldn't let me in because I was too much of a teenager so I had to hang on a doorstep all night to wait for the other lads to come out in the morning. And then we went on the road again.

We had that for about three weeks and about that time yer clothes are filthy, no change of underclothes or nothing, no place to wash, no water, nothing. The only way you had to wash was by a canal. I didn't wear socks any more, there was lumps of rough on yer feet and they was swollen, you looked a proper tramp. And I hadn't had food for days, not real food. You don't realize how much you're down, you don't realize that your health is deteriorating, your clothes is filthy, they're rags. You're down to rock-bottom, your nerves is gone.

We came to this village anyway and I went to the Catholic church, my last resort but the man said, 'We have hundreds of you people coming here all day long, we can't give you nothing and that's that.' I'd just about had enough so I said to the local copper, 'Where can I get washed like?' And he told me to go to the kip house. I went and I knocked at the door and the bloke took me upstairs to show me the bed and the smell of urine was all over the place, in chamber pots. Any clothes you had you put them under the bed. He said, 'To sleep in this place you have to have one eye open because you'll get robbed.'

In the kip house they're mostly Irish men who'd been on the road for years. They would never discuss the past but they was the first men at the bar, beer was their downfall, alcohol. At nights there was a lot of these wild men come in with the big pipes, and one night they was all round this big coal fire and I sat down and a big bloke said, 'Where's my frigging bed? If I don't get a bed,' he said, 'I'll drag yer guts out.' What they used to do was to earmark their beds with a scarf with a pincher's knot tied to the bedstead. You really had to fight for yer place some nights.

It was only from them, the old-timers, that you learned anything. They said, 'You'll have to get clothes or you'll die, you have no insulation for your body.' They all had like a duffel coat, a reefer they called it, it had big patch pockets that holds a quantity of bread, and they told me to buy meself a reefer and a cheap pair of boots. 'And all you gotta do is wear the knot at your neck and you're one of us.' They had these billy cans onto their belts and they showed me how to lubricate me shoes, fat bacon they used, so they was easier on yer feet to walk in.

You'd be okay in the kip house for a bit but then you always had to get back on the road, looking for work or something. So when one of the blokes, he was always wearing a cap at a jaunty angle and the old neck tie with the

A photograph entitled 'Down and Out on the London Embankment' taken in 1938. The embankment was one of the few places where the London County Council took a head count of the homeless population.

pincher's knot, he said, 'We're going to hit the road tomorrow so come with us.' And that's what I did.

This bloke, he was walking away in the front and he used to go into the odd verse of a song...

> *A mother's love's a blessing,*
> *Keep it while you may,*
> *For you'll never miss a mother's love,*
> *Till she's buried beneath the clay.*

Of course then the old hanky, they used to have always a red hanky, the red hanky'd come out and wipe the tears, and then he'd say a bit of swearing, pull himself out of the emotion like and he'd say, 'Pick yer bloody feet up, walk as though you mean it.' But then when it gets dark and you're sleeping out, it's then you do cry because your mind goes back to your parents, your promise. The day I left my mam I told her she'd have money next week but the money never came. The promises haunt you night after night and I couldn't contact her, nobody goes home when you're down on your uppers. You've got no money and you're filthy, you could not go back to your home.

There are always two or three of us and you know, at night, in a haystack, you sat close together for the warmth. And we all prayed for a new day, for hope and you would go to sleep and you'd dream it was there, course it wasn't in the morning. It's just walking again, trying to find a bit to eat or drink. And I was so hungry I just couldn't seem to swallow ordinary food, there was something strange about it and yet you were very, very hungry. So one of me mates told me, 'Drink milk to get you back into eating, otherwise you won't be able to digest your food.' We used to have to go into the fields and milk cows.

Course with all this I lost a lot of weight and your senses are not the same, you're not really able to debate any more, and when you come into a town you're scared of meeting people. Everybody's looking because of the way you are. I hadn't met people for weeks and weeks and weeks to talk to, only my own company and the blokes that was on the roads with me. And the walking was deadly, you didn't exist walking. Your feet would go and all you wanted was to sit down and rest. You was a dreg, you'd lost all sense of living really.

And nobody could give you a job because you couldn't present yourself. Not a proper shirt, no tie, cap, shoes. Even the farmers, they don't trust strangers or tinkers or down-and-outs or Irish. They won't allow you into their house, use the toilets, so they give you a shed of some sort, all they want is their potatoes or corn to be lifted and then they see you on your way.

One night I had to ask just to rest on at the farmyard where I'd had work for a day and I fell asleep, I was exhausted and I enjoyed my sleep, it was beautiful, a very deep sleep. During the night it rained a bit but I was happy. I was gone into a deep sleep. I didn't feel the cold, I was, I was so relaxed. I must have been on a very low ebb and during the night-time I could feel the straw being blown over my face. But what happened the next thing I knew it was dawn and there was a bloke kicking the soles of me feet. He says, 'Get up, the rats has nearly got you, they think Christmas has come.' The rats had bitten the lobes of my ears and they took what food I had in my pocket and they'd trampled over me face, but I just couldn't wake up properly. The local doctor came to try and revive me. I didn't realize what had happened but I only just made it. My ears was all blood and the blood was running down me face. And afterwards you just carried on as though nothing happened.

And my mother, she kept writing and the letters used to pile up in the kip house. It was kind of a communications' post for all the letters from home to come to. Even though you might be away, miles away, you'd always go back for your letters. But there was no money to answer them, I couldn't tell her I was a downer and a tramp, and I knew she'd be very, very worried and one day there came a letter and a pound from my dad, he must have smelt that I was well down. That was one of the big breaks because I could buy a meal, go to a café.

In the end I got a job through Costain's, the builders, because I heard they was building a huge estate. I went there with me boots on, looking really like I was used to roughing it now and all the hard work, the hard life that the builders had. I had a couple of years on the building then. Then I met me wife and we was looking to get a local council house, the first real home. But you was regimented, you couldn't come in with yer boots on. It was a different side of life. A new home, new carpet, 'Don't do this, don't do that.' And you had to live with that. You had to be recultured, keep up with the Joneses. Getting a regular job and a regular home. You didn't fit in easily, inwardly, the jump was too much. It was wonderful but it was just too much, you couldn't fit in easily."

EDDIE SLATER

Eddie was an only child, born in Gateshead in 1924. His father was an upholsterer and his mother died when Eddie was only five years old. After her death Eddie was put into the workhouse for several months until his father remarried and took his son to live with his new step-mother. In 1938 Eddie started work as a messenger boy for a dry-cleaning business. After a few months he got a job at the shipyard and when he was seventeen he joined the Merchant Navy. During the Second World War he served in the Royal Navy for three and a half years before joining the Palestine Police in 1946. When he returned to England in 1948 Eddie became a bus driver in Newcastle, then in Colchester where he met his wife. They married in 1956 and had four children. Eddie is now a widower and still lives in Colchester where he is active in Pensioners' Rights.

Eddie Slater (*front row*) and his family on a day trip to the seaside in 1931.

"I was born on the 24 May which is the old Empire Day and I used to think it was great because my birthday fell on Empire Day. It was drilled into us at school, the British Empire. On the 24th we used to have to stand in our classes and sing the national anthem and the headmaster would give us a little speech all about the Empire, how great it was and how we would have to serve it when we got older.

If we went to the pictures and saw a film like *Beau Geste* we'd come out, 'Oh, we're going to join the Foreign Legion'. We were going to join every damn thing and we used to sort of play at that sort of thing. I didn't realize that you had to have a college education for it, all I thought, 'Oh, I'm British I can get there and I'll be in the civil service and I'll be what they call an officer on the frontier.' I think childhood when we was kids was just one big make-believe. Because we couldn't get the real thing we used to pretend and live it.

All the pictures that we seen about the British Empire and the books we read was nearly all if you were an Englishman and you were white then you'd be having servants, you'd live in a big house, you'd never have to work. We were basically brought up to believe that once you went overseas your troubles finished.

The gang I belonged to, all we thought of was getting away and getting overseas, somewhere where it was nice and warm, away from all the rain and get something to eat and all. Nobody ever went on holiday or nothing like that except maybe a Sunday school trip and that was basically your life. We wanted adventure because we didn't have anything.

We couldn't visualize that it was really thousands and thousands of miles away and it would probably take you three weeks on a boat to get there. We thought we would be there if we jumped on a boat on the Monday, we'd be there Tuesday. We used to roam these ships quite happily all over the Newcastle docks and nobody used to bother us until they was leaving the harbour. We didn't give a damn where we went. Our heads had been filled that much with adventure, the great things the British Empire had done and the great things what the British Army had done. We wanted to be part of it. And we used to try by getting on the boats and running away. We would try to get to the places we had seen on the Saturday morning pictures.

When we had pinpointed a ship that we wanted to try we would gather a bottle of water and maybe some bread and dripping or anything that mum had lying around which we thought she wouldn't miss and any time we passed a fruit shop on our way we would put our hands round the corner and pinch half a dozen apples or some vegetables, a couple of carrots or something. We used to eat it all raw. We looked after each other and we fed each other, we shared everything but we never stole anything off the boats, we had a sort of a code that we didn't steal off the seamen, we'd pinch it if it was on the docks but we never pinched off the ships themselves.

Then we used to get on the boat. It was so easy because the ships used to be lying up in Newcastle docks, the river used to be full of ships in those days. With the tide coming up and down sometimes you had to jump and other times you had to go across on the ropes and find somewhere to hide. They were nearly all dirty old boats, either colliery stuff or full of pit props and this sort of thing – none of them ever carried passengers. We used to try to get to where the wheel is, the lifeboats, we used to hide in them because they used to have tarpaulins on them. Any nook or cranny, anything where we knew damn fine we were safe from anyone finding us. Lots of times we used to go to sleep because we got overpowered by the fumes of these pit props.

We had the idea the first couple of times that if you got caught then all the Captain had to do was turn round and bring us back but of course it doesn't work that way. Once you're out the breakwater they've got no communication so they just carry on their own merry way. Once the ships got through Tynemouth and the pilots had gone then we was on our own and the skipper who was the boss would say if he would put us ashore or not. Luckily most of the things that we did get on was small and they used to call in to all these ports. They probably cabled the police or the coastguard they had us aboard and they would put us off at the next stop. But we knew damn fine we'd get a good feed when we got caught and we did, they used to feed us like hell. They thought it was good that us kids wanted to join them.

All we thought about was getting somewhere foreign, our heads filled with the pictures on Saturday morning of all these foreign countries. Harry Pringle, he even got as far as Oslo and when he got back he was the hero of Gateshead. They were all buying him bubble gum and everything.

We was always trying anything to get away. And when we couldn't get on a ship we would go down the old docks. There was quite a lot of kids living on the docks in carriages on the old disused railway sidings. They was mostly orphans or kids who had run away from home.

We used to make fires there and hunt for this and that, rabbits. We never caught anything, they was too clever but we used to take spuds and roast them over the fire. We used to make little tents with anything we had, what we called dens, hidden away.

There used to be a lot of old tramps used to sleep in the trucks and they used to tell us some stories. They used to tell us the best way to cook things and how we could look after ourselves. One of these tramps taught me to sew because I'd torn me trousers and I was scared to go home. So out of this dirty old coat what he had on he brings a needle and cotton and he showed me how to sew me pants before I went home. The kids used to look after each other but it was a funny kind of life because it was so free and no fear at all, the only fear you had was getting home and getting a good hiding off your dad, which we got more than once.

We weren't supposed to be there so there was big penalties of what would happen to you if you got caught. The coppers used to come and have a look in now and then or the railway police used to look in these cars. A lot of times you got a good clout across your ear by the policeman and nobody thought of reporting them 'cos if you did you got another one from your dad.

Sometimes we'd be away for a few days, sleeping out. But now and then the policeman would take you back home after you'd only been out for a night and he used to read the riot act to dad or mum and we would all promise to be good and never do it again and then you generally got a licking either from your mum or your dad but we used to take it, never used to complain. We knew that we'd do it again, it was just part of life."

ALFRED GREGORY

Alfred, born in Chesterfield in 1930, had three sisters and one brother. Their father worked on the railway but was a heavy drinker. The family were evicted and moved from house to house throughout Alfred's childhood and he spent much of it fending for himself around Chesterfield. He didn't go to school very often and had a job on a fish and fruit stall when he was nine years old. He started working down the mines when he was fourteen in 1944. Alfred married for the first time in 1954 and had three children. This marriage ended in divorce in 1976 and he remarried his present wife in 1978. They have two children. After a pit accident in 1979 Alfred was off work for thirteen months. He was made redundant in 1985 after the miners' strike. He lives with his family in Bolsover near Chesterfield.

"There was no love as a child. I've got scars on me today where me dad threw a saucer. He was violent, he had a big army belt he'd thrash you with and he'd come in drunk, what bit of money they had he'd booze it in pubs in Chesterfield. I were just terrified of being in the house and me mother was mostly out. So I just left and slept in fields when I was about seven. I were happier under night sky, nice and quiet under there at night. You could 'ear cows munching yards away, you can hear things crawling round. Crawly things never bothered me and I used to lay in a field, perhaps with an old rug over me, for days at a time.

They reported to the police I were missing and police 'ud pick me up in a dirty dishevelled state, not much on, nothing to eat. They'd take me home and after they'd gone there'd be a row. Dad 'ud 'it me and again I'd go and it used to be like that on and off days at a time.

I only went to school when I were at home, when I were running away I didn't bother with school. I were happier freelance.

After about two years I got meself a little job on Howard's fruit and fish stall in Chesterfield market, running and fetching, and I could have as much fruit and vegetables as I wanted.

And to survive with eating, you pick things out of the hedgerow, I mean you'd pick this up off other kids, tramps, there were a lot about. I've had many a worm, they were very juicy. We was always told that they 'elp to clean yer stomach out. Horse mushrooms and Blueys wrapped in cabbage leaves 'cos that has got an anti-toxin against fungi. I was always told what a pig or fowl can eat, you can eat. I used to fill me pockets; acorns, elderberries, hawthorn haws, leaves. We'd roll them and chew them. And beech nuts, thistle nuts, sorrel leaves, very bitter but we'd chew that all. And dandelion you could nibble on root. There was a lot of allotments going about then and I'd raid them at night. Just take what you wanted, a turnip or swede, tater, carrot, beetroot. It kept me going you know.

There was some shops very good to us, cheese bits and bacon bits off slicer, little parcel of these, all the left-overs, raw bacon and raw tomato. Some shops 'ud give ya cracked eggs, broken biscuits, stuff as what had been in window too long and had softened off. Some butchers 'ud give ya a coupla sausages if you offered to clean, tidy backyard up for 'em.

I called at a farm every day and the farmer's wife 'ud give me a duck egg and I'd eat these raw. That's how you existed, how I didn't get poisoned…

I was typical little vagabond. Old jersey with the elbows out, shirt and cuffs all frayed, little and short trousers with rear end out. Never had a top coat or that. I think some people took very sad over me 'cos I were really a little blond 'aired lad, big blue eyes. I could charm some people and I learnt one or two ruses. If I had a little purse, empty and I started crying on corner of street and pretended I'd lost me mother's last few shillings some old soul 'ud come across and ask, 'What's up wi' ya duck?' And they'd make a little collection round to try and get me this money back.

The NSPCC inspector, he picked me up many times. He'd take me into the slipper baths and pay for me to have a bath, take me rags off me, wash

A derelict house in the 1930s. At this time two million or so people were living in slum conditions and in houses classified as unfit for human habitation.

them, and have 'em dried out. Then he'd take me into a café and buy me a meal, nice warm breakfast. If he couldn't find me parents he'd just give me a sixpence and tell me to take care and go.

You were lonely but you weren't lonely, if you know what I mean, you was free. There was always something fresh round next corner you know. I mean I felt a bit downhearted at some time but then the sun comes out and you start on something else.

Winter-times it was nice when it snowed 'eavy and because you could build like an igloo in a corner, scoop it out, it's very warm inside. But you got

plenty of freedom, you weren't tied down to anything, no one slapping ya down. You could come and go as you pleased and roam round.

You could lay down and see the stars till you finally dropped off to sleep through sheer exhaustion. The Plough and the North Star, things you just picked up. I used to sleep rough in Trinity churchyard 'cos nobody'd come through churchyard, not even police at night, and I'd always recite the psalm of David. I always believed that it'd look after me and I used to say, 'Yea though I walk through the valley of the shadow of death I shall fear no evil for thou art with me, thy rod and thy staff shall comfort me."

MARION NEVILLE

Marion was born in Plymouth in 1923. She had three brothers. Her father had a small business, delivering coal. Marion left school when she was sixteen and started work as a clerk at an agricultural firm. After the Blitz on Plymouth in April 1941 the family's home was destroyed and they were made homeless. They lived in their father's coal lorry for several months until they found a house to rent in Plymouth. Marion married her husband, a herdsman, in 1955. She worked as a secretary to Joan Maynard, Labour Member of Parliament, between 1978 and 1987 when she retired. She and her husband have three children and now live in Redhill, Surrey.

"It was when the light faded and you would be listening, you would hear the low hum as they were coming in. They would start with incendiary bombs and then the bombers would come. It really was just concentrated bombing and I think it was the last night we caught ours. Fortunately we were all down in the Anderson shelter. But I remember the terrible noise as it came overhead, it was as if all hell had been let loose. We didn't discover anything of

Above and left: Marion Neville and her family photographed in 1941. After their house was bombed during the Plymouth Blitz they were left homeless.

course until everything had passed over. My father had a quick look out. Then we all came up.

What I can remember is just ruins everywhere and dirt and dust and wondering who'd been killed and who'd survived. The house across the road had been hit and ours was virtually gone. Just this feeling of utter devastation, life had just suddenly crumbled. Because home is the base for everything and home is lying about you in bits. My grandmother had a beautiful mahogany bow-fronted chest and there were just bits of it, it was all smashed, and clothes and things lying there and just a feeling of helplessness. Your haven of safety has gone, you're just out on a limb, we just had a shell of a house.

It was a case of getting yourself together, see what there was to be rescued. You virtually had what you were standing up in so we put some things into boxes and my mother got bedding and shook it out well and that's how we started off from there.

We didn't feel as if we could stand any more and that's when we decided that we had to go out into the country. My father had a little business at that time, as a coal dealer with his own lorry, so we sort of cleaned it all down and we put all the things we had left in that and started driving out every night into the country, up to a village called Lee Mills. My father would pick up anybody on the way that was walking and wanted to get out of the city, sometimes there'd be two dozen people on board. A lot of them would go down to the village hall which they opened up as a sort of rest centre. But we, as a family, preferred to stay together and the lorry was better than nothing.

So we stayed in the back of the lorry. There was four of us children, my mother, my father and my grandmother. We used to space ourselves out because the lorry was fairly big. But you didn't sleep very well. You weren't able to undress, just take yer top things off and yer shoes, lay down on a blanket with a few pillows, very uncomfortable. And immediately you heard planes coming over you'd be up and looking out to see what was going on.

The main problem was washing facilities and the loo. We used to pull up in a lay-by near the village hall and so we could go in there for the toilet but in the night if you wanted to go then it meant behind a hedge.

The general feeling was one of having your dignity taken away from you.

It wasn't quite what you were used to, you wanted to get into your own bedroom and have a proper wash and clean clothes and you couldn't. Let's face it, I was eighteen and girls of that age are used to bathing and washing their hair quite frequently and being clothed and looking smart. And I was working then, in the city. To have to get up in the morning, have a wash in a bowl and just do your hair in the driving mirror of the lorry then go to work in clothes you had worn for several nights, it was not at all pleasant, very demoralizing.

The threads of your life had gone. I had a piano at home and I would go and shut myself away and sing and play, that was gone, your books, being able to get home and relax. I think I did resent that. And the way you were just left to put up with it. You just had a sense of isolation, of floating, of not belonging anywhere. I know a house is only a building, but a home is a home, it's something that you need, everybody needs that, to be able to go in and shut your own front door and be at home."

Left and below: **Marion and her family were forced to live in her father's lorry for several months.**

RENIE LESTER

Renie was born in 1924 in Manchester. Her parents divorced when she was three years old and she was then cared for by her grandfather who was a mechanic. When she was fourteen Renie started work in the Co-op mineral water factory and then went into the cotton mill a year later. She married her husband, who was dyer in a printing factory, when she was eighteen.

During the Second World War Renie's husband was a stoker on a Royal Navy destroyer. When he returned from the war in 1945 he found work in the steel works in Scunthorpe. Unable to find anywhere to live Renie, her husband and her children had to lodge at her parents' home. In 1946, after living there for a year, the family became one of the first families to squat in the disused army camp at Sawcliffe. They lived there in a Nissen hut for two years. They were then given a condemned cottage to live in until they were finally given a council house in 1951. Renie has six children and now lives in Scunthorpe.

Left: Renie Lester and her husband at the beginning of the Second World War.
They were to become two of Britain's first squatters.
Above: Renie Lester and one of her children pictured in 1947.

"We was living with me mother, me dad, me grandfather, in the same house, me, me husband, two kiddies, overcrowded. You couldn't get rooms nowhere you see, because all the servicemen were coming 'ome. All the houses had been bombed and there'd been no building, no nothing. You couldn't have a row, you'd to have a row in a fierce whisper, you know. Anyway we managed for so long then we got to 'ear that this camp was being taken over, it was a disused army camp.

There was no water turned on, there was no electric turned on, there was no proper roads, it was just mud paths. No amenities at all but we decided we'd pack up and go and live in there. We had this 'orse and cart and all I had was a tub and a chair and a coupla tables and a cot.

We divided our hut off into bedrooms and a little kitchen with our bedspreads and our curtains. You couldn't see through the windows, they was 'igh up, meshed. Stone floor, flags, you could buy Cardinal polish them days, it was red. No proper roads, if it wasn't dry it was mud. But we decided to call it Freedom Avenue because we was free at long last and we stencilled a board and put it at the top of the road. We was proud of each other at the camp because we was all in the same boat, we were all genuinely wanting 'omes. And we thought if they came to turn us off we'd lie on the road. If they wanted to put us in jail they would have to put us all in jail. We decided we was gonna stick there.

It was a struggle from morning till night, it was really, really rough and you felt like giving up. Pouring with rain, maybe snowing, maybe blowing and there was no coal and it were bitter cold 'cos we had a very, very bad winter. There's like two sheets of steel for a roof and you'd lie in bed and you'd 'ear rats running in between. We kept camp going more or less but it was very 'ard.

We was burying rubbish and covering it over, we'd toilets that stunk to heck because you couldn't flush 'em. Fumes from the paraffin lamps got in yer clothes, got in yer skin. We wanted to have water put on because the toilets was there, there was electric there but for some reason the Council didn't want to help us. We had to go beg water and we made ourselves nuisances, keep knocking on doors. Ya felt dirty because you 'adn't had a wash from morning. You felt dirty, you felt grubby. The men couldn't shave as often as they wanted to shave, had to go a bit scruffy. And if anybody came for a cup of tea they used to bring a pot bottle full of water. My mother didn't live too far away so at least I could go once a week and bath all the kids and have a bath meself.

Then they decided that they'd open this reservoir and we could get our water from there. We had a white bucket but you couldn't 'ardly walk you see, it had snowed and froze over the top, couldn't keep yer balance. I was pregnant at the time with me eldest son and when 'e was born I had nothing but melted snow for 'im, it's no wonder there was sickness like there were. We'd buckets of melted snow, that's all we 'ad. Eventually I took that poorly that they had to take me into hospital and the baby had to come with me 'cos I was breast-feeding.

It was 'ard and people looked down on ya because you was like gypsies. They looked down their nose at ya if you caught the bus, everything went dead quiet. I begrudged 'em their 'ouses, the smug, complacent little gardens. You was dirt, you was rubbish, they didn't give you a chance. We was genuine people who were wanting to be with our husbands, wanting to make our lives all over. We was trying to make these 'uts into 'omes, put curtains up, always changing furniture round to make 'em look posh. Pincha few flowers, only out of 'edges, put them in the window in a milk bottle. We would have been thankful to live in a kennel, to live with our men, but they had no sympathy for us. We were only trying to make 'omes but we felt outcasts.

We was just unfortunate that we 'adn't got 'omes, we weren't, we weren't asking for summat for nowt, we'd worked for our 'omes, we worked for that 'ut, gone through 'ardships. We'd been parted from our 'usbands, we'd been bombed, we'd been shot at."

JANICE COOKE

Janice was born in Southend-on-Sea in 1944. She was adopted a year later in 1945 and brought up in Peckham, South London, with one brother. Her adoptive father was an advertising clerk for a whisky company. He sexually abused Janice throughout her childhood from when she was about three. In 1957 Janice began to play truant from school and run away from home. When she was sixteen she ran away to Blackpool and slept rough for two weeks. The police returned her to London but her parents refused to take her back and she was put into various children's homes in south-east London over the next year. From there Janice was put into St Ebbw's Mental Hospital where she remained for two years. During this time her mother died and she lost all contact with her father.

When she was released in 1962 Janice went to live in London and supported herself by working as a prostitute. Her first child was born in 1965 and she went on to have two more children. She was married in 1979 but was divorced five years later. In 1985 Janice met her second husband at the Post Office where they both worked and they moved to Exeter together. They married in January 1994. Janice has just finished writing her autobiographical novel, Peckham Cry.

Janice Cooke in 1955. Janice ran away from home and slept rough in Blackpool when she was only sixteen.

"I can remember at the age of two or three being abused by my father. When he used to talcum powder me he used to fondle me but as I grew older it gradually grew more and more intense and he asked me to do certain things to him. He used to give me a threepenny bit to tell nobody. I began to dread going home from school.

When I was sixteen I had to leave school, much to my disappointment because I desperately wanted to stay on, and the sexual abuse was still going on. I was so unhappy that I decided to sit down and talk to my mother about it and I told her exactly what had been going on. She didn't believe me. She really went for me like a mad woman, sent me up to bed and when my father came home that night there was a big argument because she confronted him. And he said that he'd never touched me. He came up and beat me, my mother screamed at me and she got my head between her hands and started banging it against the wall, and she scratched me. And she said to me, 'Get out the house'. So I said, 'Well, I'll go anyway.' I decided then that I'd had enough.

I had some money saved in a bottle in my room so about ten o'clock I crept out of the house. I wandered around London trying to think of somewhere to go. At the time I was in the Frankie Vaughan fan club, I thought he was wonderful and I spent a lot of time listening to his records. As I was walking round that night I realized that Frankie Vaughan was in Blackpool for the summer season. I decided to go there.

At King's Cross I bought a tuppenny platform ticket and I got on a train, slept most of the journey up there. Luckily I wasn't disturbed by the ticket inspector. At the other end I shot out through the gate, the barrier, and there I was in Blackpool. And I was frightened. I wanted to see Frankie Vaughan but I was frightened to go to the theatre so I wandered around Blackpool aimlessly.

I thought I'd try and find somewhere to stay so I went to the Social Security and they said, 'Well if you haven't got a fixed address then you can't have any money.' I'd got nowhere to stay and I'd got no money. I didn't dare tell anyone I'd run away from home. So that night I slept under the pier where it was dry.

In the morning I wandered around again. There was still a lot of holidaymakers up there and I looked at people with their children walking hand-in-hand going in the amusement arcades, all lit up, and the silly noises, and the people putting pennies in the slots. I went in and stood next to a little girl and started talking to her and she said she was on holiday with her parents and I thought how lucky she was.

I went on sleeping rough for about a fortnight and all that time I didn't have any food. I think I went down to the shore and started drinking some of the salty water but that made me sick. I was dirty, I was smelly and I didn't really care what I looked like. I'd wet my knickers because I hadn't taken any clothes with me. I was going into the toilets and trying to have a bit of a wash and brush up but I felt like dying because I had nowhere to go, nobody wanted to know, nobody wanted me at home, don't think they ever did.

I pinched a sponge, a bath sponge, from one of the shops along the front, it was round and it was orange. I thought it was an orange and I started to try to peel it as if to eat it. In actual fact I was just suffering from delirium. I'd had nothing to eat, I'd had nothing to drink for two weeks. The next thing I remember is a light shining in my eyes and a policeman saying, 'Hullo, what are you doing under there?' And I think at the time I was relieved to see him and yet I was scared as well. I felt that maybe I'd been saved, he might listen to me.

Above: Janice Cooke in the early 1960s shortly after being
released from St Ebbw's Mental Institution.
Right: Janice Cooke's father photographed in the 1940s.

The police sent me back to London and they contacted my parents and
they didn't want to know. The next thing I knew they were placing me in care
of the LCC, in a children's home in Blackheath and it was quite nice there. I
was the oldest child so I didn't get beaten up. It was there that I learnt that my
mother had died of a heart attack.

I started running away from the home and sleeping out nights 'til
eventually the authorities decided that for my own protection I should be put
somewhere more secure, and that's how I found myself at this hospital in
Epsom. It frightened the living daylights out of me. It was a mental hospital.

I spent two years in this hospital and by that time I was institutionalized
and I didn't really want to go outside and face the outside world. But they
decided it was time that I set out on my own. I didn't have much confidence
but they found me a hostel in Chelsea and I found myself a job.

But I was struggling to pay me rent at this hostel where I was stopping and
I kept thinking back to when I was homeless and dreading that happening
again really. One night when I was coming back from work I turned round the
corner and a man approached me and asked if I did business. He said, 'I'll put it
bluntly, do you go to bed with men for money?' He offered to give me three

pounds and I thought about it and I thought, 'Oh, well why not?' And I took him back and it was all over in a coupla minutes. I had a bath after he went and I didn't think anything of it, and there I was three pounds richer. And that really started me off on prostitution.

I didn't do it on any big scale, I was never brazen enough to stand there and say, 'Hullo darlin', how about a good time?' I used to wander around and pretend I was nonchalantly looking at something else, but if I saw somebody that looked nice, probably some elderly gentleman that I didn't think could do me any harm, I'd walk over. But I was always very shy and nervous. I always used to put the lights off and I used to bath before and afterwards as if trying to rub the dirt off of me, but it was, it was a job. I didn't have feelings for them, in fact I didn't have feelings for anybody so I just felt numb. I didn't have feelings for myself, I didn't have a high opinion of myself so it didn't really matter how I felt."

FURTHER READING

ADDISON, P.   *Now the war is over: a social history of Britain, 1945–51*, J. Cape 1985.

BAILEY, V.   *Delinquency and citizenship: reclaiming the young offender, 1914–48*, Oxford U.P., 1987.

BELCHEM, J. ed.   *Popular politics, riot and labour: essays in Liverpool history, 1790–1940*, Liverpool U.P., 1992.

BRISTOW, E.   *Vice and vigilance: purity movements in Britain since 1700*, Dublin Gill and Macmillan, 1977. op.

BURT, C.   *The young delinquent*, University of London Press, 1944.

BUSCHKE, A. & JACOBSOHN, F.   *Introduction to sexual hygiene*, Routledge, 1932. op.

COLLEDGE, D.   *Labour camps: the British experience*, Sheffield Popular Publishing, 1989.

COSTELLO, J.   *Love, sex and war: changing values, 1939–1945*, Collins, 1985. op.

CROUCHER, R.   *We refuse to starve in silence: a history of the National Unemployed Workers' Movement*, Lawrence and Wishart, 1987.

DUNNING, E. et al.   *The roots of football hooliganism*, Routledge, 1988; pbk, 1990.

FERGUSON, H.   'Cleveland in history: the abused child and child protection, 1880–1914' in Cooter, R. ed. *In the name of the child: health and welfare, 1800–1940*, Routledge, 1992.

FIELD, J.   *Learning through labour: training, education and the state, 1890–1939*, University of Leeds, 1991.

FRYER, P.   *Staying power: the history of black people in Britain*, Pluto Press, 1984.

GILLIS, J.   *For better, for worse: British marriages, 1600 to the present*, Oxford U. P., 1985.

HASTE, C.   *Rules of desire: sex in Britain since World War I*, Chatto, 1992.

HUMPHRIES, S. et al.   *A century of childhood*, Sidgwick and Jackson, 1988. op.

HUMPHRIES, S.   *Hooligans or rebels?: an oral history of working class childhood and youth, 1889–1939*, Oxford; Blackwell, 1981. op.

HUMPHRIES, S.   *A secret world of sex: forbidden fruit – the British experience, 1900–50*, Sidgwick and Jackson, 1989.

HYAM, R.   *Empire and sexuality: the British experience*, Manchester U.P., 1991.

KOHN, M.   *Dope girls: birth of the British drug underground*, Lawrence and Wishart, 1992.

LAWSON, A.   *Adultery: an analysis of love and betrayal*, Oxford U.P., 1990.

LEWIS, J.   *Women in England, 1870–1950: sexual divisions and social change,* Harvester Wheatsheaf, 1984.

LUDOVICI, A.   *Woman: a vindication,* Constable, 1923. op.

MACINTYRE, S.   *Little Moscows: communism and working-class militancy in inter-war Britain,* Croom Helm, 1980. op.

MACK, J. &   *London at war: the making of modern London, 1939–1945,* HUMPHRIES, S.   Sidgwick and Jackson, 1985. op.

MINNS, R.   *Bombers and mash: the domestic front, 1939–1945,* Virago, 1980. op.

MURRAY, B.   *The old firm: sectarianism, sport and society in Scotland,* Edinburgh; J. Donald, 1984. op.

ORWELL, G.   *Down and out in Paris and London,* Penguin, 1933.

PANAYI, P. ED.   *Racial violence in Britain, 1840–1950,* Leicester U.P., 1993.

PEARSON, G.   *Hooligan: a history of respectable fears,* Macmillan, 1983.

RICHARDS, M. &   *Sexual arrangements: marriage and affairs,* Heinemann, 1992; REIBSTEIN, J.   Mandarin, 1993.

ROSE, L.   *Rogues and vagabonds: vagrant underworld in Britain, 1815–1985,* Routledge, 1988 op.

ROTHSTEIN, A.   *The soldiers' strikes of 1919,* Journeyman Press, 1985.

SCHWARTZ,   *Child sexual abuse: the initial effects,* Sage, 1990. B. GOMES et al.

SMITHIES, E.   *Crime in wartime: a social history of crime in World War II,* Allen and Unwin, 1982.

STONE, L.   *The road to divorce: England, 1530–1987,* Oxford U.P., 1992.

WADDINGTON, D.   *Contemporary issues in public disorder: a comparative and historical approach,* Routledge, 1992.

WATSON, S. &   *Housing and homelessness: a feminist perspective,* Routledge, 1986. AUSTERBERRY, H.

WEEKS, J.   *Sex, politics and society: the regulation of sexuality since 1800,* Longman, 1989.

WHITE, J.   'The riots in perspective: the summer riots of 1919' in *New Society,* 13 August 1981, pp. 260–261.

WYATT, G. E. &   *Lasting effects of child sexual abuse,* Sage, 1988. POWELL, G. J.

If you are interested in oral history and collecting the memories of older people, you can join the Oral History Society which holds regular meetings, provides advice on how to interview and publishes a twice yearly magazine. Write to: Rob Perks, Curator of Oral History, National Sound Archive, 29 Exhibition Road, London SW7 2AS.

INDEX

Page numbers in bold denote illustrations.
References regarding the 'war' refer to the
Second World War unless otherwise specified.

ACKNOWLEDGEMENTS

We would like to thank all those who have helped us in writing this book. We are indebted to Sheila Ableman, Anna Ottewill, Frank Phillips, Jo Wiese, Judith Robertson and Deirdre O'Day of BBC Books for their advice and support. Special thanks to Sam Organ and Peter Grimsdale of BBC Bristol for their valuable contribution to the television series which this book accompanies. Thanks to Paul Thompson for his comments on reading the draft of this book.

Thanks also to Sharon Tanton, Gary Armstrong, Rebecca Leathlean, Steve Grogan, Brian Pedley, Frank Critchlow, Mary Parsons, Harry Ferguson, John Field, Rob Perks, Rob Wilkinson, Maggi Cook, George Matthews, Madge Reed, Lola Hardingham, Mike Humphries, Marilyn Davis, Nicolas Pronay, Stephen Bourne, Bob Little, Jude Howells, Edwin Banks, Angela and Alan Watson, Alba Crawley, Stephen and Olive Peet, Doris Bailey, Andy Cole, Steve Haskett, Nick Dance, Daniel de Waal, Fred Hart, Andy Attenburrow, Jan Faull and the ever-helpful staff of the National Film and Television Archive, the Communist Party of Great Britain, the Democratic Left, *The Big Issue* (London Office) and BBC Bristol Reference Library for all the help they have given us on the book and the series.

Finally we are deeply indebted to all the people who spoke to us and whose memories form the core of this book.

PICTURE CREDITS

BBC Books would like to thank the following for providing photographs and for permission to reproduce copyright material. While every effort has been made to trace and acknowledge all copyright holders, we would like to apologize should there have been any errors or omissions.

Page 5, Hulton Deutsch Collection Ltd; 7, British Film Institute; 10–11, The Salvation Army; 12, by Courtesy of Edinburgh City Libraries; 15, 18–19, British Film Institute; 21, W. F. Lestrange, *Wasted Lives*, Routledge, 1936, p. 111; 24, 26, Larry Rankin; 31, Hulton Deutsch Collection Ltd; 34–35, Dundee District Library; 43, British Film Institute; 44–45, 49, 53, 54, 59, Hulton Deutsch Collection Ltd; 60, 61, Marjorie Hopkins; 63, 65, 66, Alison Pierson; 70, Hulton Deutsch Collection Ltd; 73, The Royal Photographic Society, Bath; 74, Alison Ashford; 75, Hulton Deutsch Collection Ltd; 77, Barbara Baker; 78–79, Camera Press, photo: Peter Miles; 82, Hulton Deutsch Collection Ltd; 85, Mary Evans Picture Library; 88–89, Topham; 91, 92–93, Communist Party Library; 95, 96 Hulton Deutsch Collection Ltd; 98–99, 100, Freda Philp; 102, The Illustrated London News Picture Library; 108–109, Charlie Goodman; 111, Hulton Deutsch Collection Ltd; 114–115, 118–119, Communist Party Library; 121, Hulton Deutsch Collection; 124–125, Communist Party Library; 128, Hulton Deutsch Collection; 133, Kate Reynolds; 136–137, Communist Party Library; 139, Ben Russ; 142, May Rogers; 147, Communist Party Library; 148, The Plebs League/Blackfriars Press Ltd; 152 (above), NSPCC Archive, Accession No: 198/3/1; 152 (below), NSPCC Archive; 154–155, The Rohauer Collection/British Film Institute; 159–160, Sylvia Baardwyk; 163, 165, Maud Wood; 173, 175, Carole Mandeville; 178–179, Hulton Deutsch Collection Ltd; 181, Dundee District Library; 182–183, 184, Communist Party Library; 186–187, The Salvation Army; 189, Barnardo's Photographic Archive; 190, Hulton Deutsch Collection Ltd; 193, John Neary; 196, Hulton Deutsch Collection Ltd; 199, Eddie Slater; 204–205, Communist Party Library; 206, 207, 208, 209, Marion Neville; 210, 211, Renie Lester; 214, 216, 217, Janice Cooke.